AMONG THE
THE
MAYA
RUINS

RAND McNALLY BOOKS

by Ann and Myron Sutton

STELLER OF THE NORTH

EXPLORING WITH THE BARTRAMS

JOURNEY INTO ICE: *John Franklin and the Northwest Passage*

ANIMALS ON THE MOVE: *The Story of Migration*

AMONG THE MAYA RUINS

By ANN AND MYRON SUTTON

The Adventures of
John Lloyd Stephens and
Frederick Catherwood

Illustrated with Photographs

RAND McNALLY & COMPANY

To Elizabeth Hambleton

CONTENTS

ILLUSTRATIONS

Illustrations

MAPS

INTRODUCTION

THIS book is about two skillful, patient, and methodical explorers who more than a century ago traveled in dangerous and unknown regions of Central America. It is also about the ancient Maya Indians whose cities they explored and made known to the world.

From the moment John Lloyd Stephens and his partner, Frederick Catherwood, stepped into the jungles of Guatemala, their adventures began. In a war-torn land, where battles often raged, they carefully, even coolly, explored the ruins and buried cities. From their pens came the world's first accurate descriptions and drawings of a vanished culture whose accomplishments seem more remarkable with each passing year.

Any summary of the lives of Stephens and Catherwood can hardly do justice to all their activities—where adventures crowd on adventures. So elegantly expressed were Stephens' thoughts that they almost demand to be quoted frequently, yet there is not room here for even a tenth of them. Catherwood's magnificent drawings, likewise, are too many to be included fully in this book. In places we have emphasized the drama of a scene by dialogue taken almost verbatim from Stephens' journals, or have expressed his "thoughts" in words and phrases actually used by him in his published writings. For a more detailed study, one can still consult Stephens' works, which are well illustrated by Catherwood and are listed in the Bibliography on page 203. For a full biography of Stephens and his world, and for detailed interpretations of the Mayas and their various worlds, no one should miss the works of Victor W. von Hagen, listed also on page 204.

Of the ruins that Stephens and Catherwood visited, some are well preserved, while others are gradually disappearing with time. We followed portions of the Stephens-Catherwood trail in Guatemala, Honduras, and Mexico and came to understand, at least in part, why both men were so impressed with what they saw. We had a great deal of competent help, which Stephens usually lacked. Special thanks go to our good friend, Sr. Jorge Ibarra, Director of the National Museum of Natural History, Guatemala City, whose assistance was crucial, and who read the manuscript to check for accuracy. He did his job well, and so did others who reviewed all or parts of the manuscript, and any remaining errors are ours.

Grateful thanks are also due José Pereira, Rufino Quan, Lucy Sturgill, James and Matilda Metcalf, Maria Buchinger, John Corbett, and Gordon R. Willey.

To explore the Maya ruins is one of the greatest of thrills; and to go with Stephens and Catherwood—devoted and inspired guides that they are—is to live again that great adventure, during which the wonders of the Mayas were first unveiled.

Ann and Myron Sutton
Alexandria, Virginia

1

"MULA!"

O

"HO! Mula! Ándale! Ándale!"

The rain-soaked jungle was not quiet today. The ordinary gloom was shattered by the crack of whips, by the splashing of mules as they struggled up the stream bed, and by shouts and curses of muleteers.

"Cuidado! Cuidado! Vámonos!"

The brown skin of the men glistened with beads of rain and sweat. The muleteers, shirtless, trousers rolled above the knees, splashed among the mules—pulling them out of the mud, leaping after strays, catching a load that was about to fall, or propping their feet against the side of a mule and pulling with gusto to tighten a carrying strap.

Seeking a muddy path through the mountain forest came the Indians, naked except for a cloth around their hips. On their backs they carried heavy loads that were held by a supporting strap across the forehead.

Over at the side two white men slipped and stumbled along, each armed with a brace of pistols and a hunting knife carried in a belt. Their faces were wet with sweat, their tunics spattered, their trousers caked with mud.

One, a spare but distinguished-looking man of forty, pulled to a stop, looked at his companion with a sigh of despair, and said: "If I had known of this mountain, you might have come to Central America alone!"

The other, a younger man, brown-eyed, slender, well-dressed, was muddy from head to foot. The beard, and what you could see of his hair, were dark red.

"Mr. Catherwood," he said, propping himself against a

11

stump, "I have been thinking and composing as we walked through these wretched mudholes."

"Composing?" Catherwood asked.

"Yes. Our epitaph."

Catherwood smiled weakly. "And what will it say?"

"Tossed over the head of a mule, brained by the trunk of a mahogany tree, and buried in the mud of Mico Mountain."

Laughing, they turned up the trail. But the rocks and roots were too slippery, and the slope too steep, to proceed on foot. Back on their mules they climbed—for better or worse.

Behind rode Augustin, a young French Spaniard, armed with pistols and a sword. After Augustin staggered the pack mules, and then came four native Indians bent under heavy loads.

Of the three muleteers attached to their little party, the chief one rode a mule and carried a machete, its wide, sharp, sword-like blade occasionally reflecting the dull light of the clouded sky. Two other muleteers, each with a gun, walked, or stumbled, alongside.

The main caravan, consisting of nearly a hundred mules and their riders, had gone ahead, and the little party now increased its pace. No easy job, this: everywhere were puddles of water and pools of mud as deep as the fetlocks of the mules.

Giant mahogany trees hung over the trail. Their roots, not round like the roots of other trees, but sharply edged, criss-crossed and protruded into the path. This made it especially difficult for the mules to pick their way upward.

In places, rushing streams had deepened the path into narrow defiles, or gullies, that rose above the heads of the riders. Squeezing into these, the mules fell against the muddy sides, pinning the legs of the riders.

Despite all hardships, however, the caravan slowly and

noisily made its way up the mountain. At one point, it was met by a tall dark man who wore a broad-brimmed Panama hat, striped jacket, plaid trousers, spurs, and sword. He was as encrusted with mud as Catherwood and the bearded man.

The stranger hailed them in English and introduced himself as a businessman who had been in Guatemala City to see about establishing a bank. He shook hands with Catherwood and with the younger, red-haired man, who said that his name was John Lloyd Stephens and that he was an official of the United States Government.

They wanted to talk a long time with the businessman about the country into which they were going, but time and the caravan did not stand still. There were many more miles to go that day. So they chatted only briefly, then said good-by and moved on.

If anything, the trail became worse the higher they went. "Heavy rains from which we had suffered at sea," Stephens wrote in describing the journey, "had deluged the mountain, and it was in the worst state it could be and still be passable; sometimes it was not passable at all. . . .

"The mules were only half loaded, but, even so, several broke down and the lash could not move them; scarcely one passed over the mountain without a fall. Of our immediate party, mine fell first. Finding that I could not save her with the rein, by an exertion that strained every nerve I lifted myself from off her back and flung myself clear of roots and trees (but not of mud) to discover I had escaped an even worse danger: my dagger had fallen from its sheath and was standing upright with the handle in the mud, a foot of naked blade.

"Then Mr. Catherwood, too, was thrown from his mule with such violence that for a few moments, feeling the helplessness of our condition, I was horror-struck. . . .

"Shortly after, Augustin's mule fell backward; he kicked

John Lloyd Stephens, about 1840; age about 35

his feet out of the stirrups and attempted to slide off behind, but the mule rolled and caught him with his left leg under. But for his kicking, I should have thought that every bone in his body was broken, and the mule kicked worse than he. But they rose together and without any damage, except that the mud, which before lay upon them in spots, was now formed into a regular plaster."

Back on the mule, lurching in the saddle, hanging on with all his strength, Stephens recalled the muddy roads of New York when the spring thaw came each year. As a boy, he had gone riding along those roads, but never through such a morass as this on Mico Mountain.

Nowhere in his travels had he seen such mud—not in Greece, not in England, not in France, or Russia, or Italy, or Egypt, and certainly not in Arabia, where he had been the first American to visit the fabled ruins of Petra. That had been three years ago, in 1836. What a difference between the two lands! Arabia was as dry as Guatemala was wet.

Nor had Stephens seen the like of this when, at the age of seven (he was born on November 28, 1805), he and hundreds of other boys in nankeen pantaloons watched the preparations for the defense of New York City against the British in 1812, or when, much later, he and his cousin John rode a covered wagon from New York to Pittsburgh one summer, then took a keelboat down the Ohio River to Illinois, and a steamboat down the Mississippi River to New Orleans. Those had been tame journeys!

The mules continued to stumble and slide, winding their way along the streams and muddy trails toward the top of Mico Mountain. Mists rose from the dense tangle of forest that hemmed them in on every side. Monkeys chattered and howled in the trees.

At one o'clock, to Stephens' great satisfaction, they reached the summit. What a climb it had been! If their entire trip were to be over roads such as that, they would never get to Guatemala City.

After a few minutes' rest, the air rang with shouts of muleteers; once more, with crack of whip, they forced their mules onto the trail. But now the way was down instead of up. As men and animals slipped and slid, Stephens was convinced that the muleteers were trying to tumble the mules down the mountainside in as short a time as possible.

Watching the mule in front of him placing its feet among the roots and stones, he wondered: "Could this be the great high road to Guatemala City?" The relative comfort of the brig *Mary Ann*, which had brought him and Catherwood from New York to Belize, in what is now British Honduras, had not prepared him for this. Hurried on by a favorable northeast wind, the ship had made good time and the journey had been interesting and pleasant.

After a brief stay in Belize they had embarked in an old steamboat which took them south to the Carib Indian settlement of Punta Gorda. Here they saw leaf-thatched Indian huts along the bank, shaded by groves of coconut trees. "Canoes with sails set were lying on the water," Stephens wrote, "and men and women were sitting under the trees gazing at us. It was a soft and sunny scene, speaking peace and freedom from the tumults of a busy world."

They had then floated up the Río Dulce, one of the most beautiful rivers in Central America. "On each side," he wrote, "rising perpendicularly from three to four hundred feet, was a wall of living green. Trees grew from the water's edge with dense, unbroken foliage to the top. . . . On both sides, from the tops of the highest trees, long tendrils descended to the water, as if to drink and carry life to the trunks that bore them. . . .

"As we advanced, the passage turned, and in a few minutes we lost sight of the sea and were enclosed on all sides by a forest wall; but the river, although showing us no passage, still invited us onward. Could this be the portal to a land of volcanoes and earthquakes, to one torn and distracted by civil war?

"From the fanciful accounts we had heard we expected to see monkeys gamboling among the trees and parrots flying over our heads, but all was as quiet as if man had never been here before. The pelican, the stillest of birds, was the only living thing we saw, and the only sound was the unnatural bluster of our steam engine. . . .

"For nine miles the passage continued thus, one scene of unvarying beauty, then suddenly the narrow river expanded into a large lake, encompassed by mountains and studded with islands, which the setting sun illuminated with gorgeous splendor. We remained on deck till a late hour, and awoke the next morning in the harbor of Izabal."

Stephens had had no suspicion of what lay ahead when he had strolled the main street of Belize, enjoying the balmy breezes of November. Punta Gorda and Izabal, too, seemed like almost any other peaceful village. The people were handsome, their skins black and smooth as velvet. The men wore hats of straw and white cotton shirts and trousers. The women, attired in short-sleeved dresses of white with red borders, were adorned with large red earrings and necklaces.

Up here on the high road there was none of that. The travel and merchandise of Europe passed this way, and the feet of countless mules had trampled the road into an awful condition.

By some miracle, the guide carrying Stephens' barometer had kept the delicate instrument unbroken. But the mercury had leaked out, and there was no possibility of refilling it in Guatemala. Stephens felt the loss keenly. How much he had wanted to use it to measure altitudes. The heights of many of the mountains in the direction they were heading toward had never been measured.

Down they went. Tumbling and pitching along the
trail, they came to cascading wild rivers, the rushing tor-
rents of which they had to wade. At last they reached a
level land, thickly wooded with groves of palm trees.

Now beneath the soft, blue tropical sky, Stephens and
Catherwood were reminded of riding along the Nile River
of Egypt. It had been Catherwood's drawings of ancient
Egyptian temples that had deeply impressed Stephens.

Catherwood, six years the elder, was taller and more
solidly built. A Scot by descent, but born in London on
February 27, 1799, he had light hair, blue eyes, and a
round face, and though always enthusiastic, he usually remained quiet and reserved. His training as an artist and
an architect had made him acquainted with, and an admirer
of, the paintings of Giovanni Piranesi, a noted eighteenth-
century engraver who had so beautifully, even mysteriously,
brought to life the ancient cities of Rome.

In 1821 Catherwood had gone to Rome, then to Egypt,
then to the Middle East. He had been employed to repair
the mosques of Cairo, and it was he who first made widely
known the ruins of Baalbec, in what is now the Republic
of Lebanon. He had also been the first trained architect to
draw many of the ruins of Egypt.

At a London exhibition of four of his large panoramic
canvases of the city of Jerusalem, Catherwood and Stephens
had met. While talking about their separate adventures in
the Middle East, Catherwood showed Stephens a book describing ancient ruins on another continent—North America.
Very little was known of the ruins of Guatemala. Not many
men had seen them, and fewer still had brought back drawings of them. Mostly there were only legends, stories of lost
cities, and tales of a once-great civilization of Maya Indians.

Stephens had read what little there was in print about
these mysterious ruins in the jungles of Central America.

Hammock similar to those used by Stephens and his party

And even before he had met Catherwood, others had urged him to explore the lost kingdoms of the Mayas.

But why? Had he wished, Stephens could have followed three other careers. He was a successful New York lawyer. He was a politician, and since he had done a great deal to get Martin Van Buren elected President of the United States, he might have had an important position in government. Or, as an author, his future had been assured by the success of his books, *Incidents of Travel in Egypt, Arabia Petraea, and the Holy Land,* published in 1837, and *Incidents of Travel in Greece, Turkey, Russia, and Poland,* published in 1838.

History does not tell exactly why Stephens hired Catherwood to accompany him on this expedition. Ostensibly there was a secret mission for President Van Buren. But we can suppose that curiosity drew them together, as well as the lure of lost cities and the love of adventure. All we know is that shortly after Stephens and Catherwood met they were partners in exploration, journeying into the interior of a wild and unknown land.

Toward dark of the first day, they reached a *rancho,* a small house constructed of poles and plastered with mud. They, too, were plastered with mud, from head to foot, and dead tired. Yet they talked with other travelers at the rancho and in so doing completely forgot to retrieve fresh clothes from their baggage before the muleteers retired.

They hung up their hammocks and turned in as they were, with stiff and muddy clothes, uncomfortable in the extreme. But neither this nor the buzzing of insects could keep them from sleep.

Next day they were on the move again. The main caravan had gone on, and now their little party traveled by itself. The country through which they passed was far more appealing than that of the day before. Their first view of the Motagua River, seen from a high ridge, prompted Stephens to describe the river as one of the noblest in Central America. It was wide and gently winding, with long mudbanks and sandy stretches often occupied by large white birds. The jungle came to the edge of it in many places, yet the valley through which the Motagua flowed had a desert aspect, with towering cactuses on the hillsides.

"We saw the Motagua River, one of the noblest in Central

Higher, along the slopes of thickly forested ridges, roaring white cascades poured into the valley.

"It was one of the most beautiful scenes I ever beheld," Stephens wrote. "All around were giant mountains, and the river, broad and deep, rolled through them with the force of a mighty torrent."

Climbing into the mountains, they rode through villages of plastered and whitewashed houses that had piazzas, or verandas, and balconied windows. Every village, it seemed, possessed a church. Wherever he could, Stephens visited the priest, or *cura*, from whom he got information about the country and the people.

From time to time a detachment of soldiers marched by, with muskets shining ominously—a reminder of the state of revolution the country was in. Stephens had been warned that the road to Guatemala City was occupied by troops and that trouble might come. It did.

America, rolling majestically through the valley . . ."

2

STRANGE MISSION

O O

AT six o'clock one evening they came to what appeared to be a deserted village. In an abandoned building, which they deemed as good a place as any to spend the night, they prepared their supper.

But the village was not deserted, and the Indian *alcalde* (mayor) and several *alguaciles* (policemen) came to watch the proceedings of the strangers. After a while, apparently satisfied, they went away.

The *cabildo,* or building in which the travelers had taken refuge for the night, was about forty feet long and twenty feet wide, with plastered walls into which pegs had been placed for the attachment of hammocks.

"Mr. Catherwood was in his hammock," as Stephens remembered the events of that night, "and I was half undressed when the door was suddenly burst open and twenty-five or thirty men rushed in, the *alcalde, alguaciles,* soldiers, Indians, and *mestizos* (persons of mixed Indian and Spanish origin), ragged and ferocious-looking fellows armed with staves of office, swords, clubs, machetes, and carrying blazing pine sticks."

The *alcalde* no longer had a smile on his face.

"*Pasaporte!*" he demanded.

Stephens handed over his passport, which was in turn passed to the captain, who stood scowling, hand on sword. The captain examined the passport briefly and gave it back to Stephens, saying:

"Not valid. It is signed by the general of another province. It must have the seal of the State of Guatemala."

"I was not very familiar with the Spanish language," Stephens wrote later, "but, using Augustin as interpreter, I attempted to explain. . . . The *alcalde* paid no attention to my explanations; he said that he had seen a passport once before and that it had been printed on a small piece of paper not bigger than his hand, unlike mine, which had been issued by the government on a quarto sheet."

Stephens explained that he was a special envoy from the President of the United States (*del Norte,* as the Guatemaltecos called the land to the north). He said that he was entrusted with a special confidential mission to the United States of Central America and that the purpose of his trip was to ascertain the whereabouts of the government of Central America.

"You cannot go on," the captain replied. "You will stay in this village."

The *alcalde* remained silent. Stephens explained that delay of a diplomatic officer could lead to serious consequences. The captain seemed unimpressed.

"Give me your passport," he demanded, apparently deciding that he would keep the passport after all.

At this, Stephens drew himself up proudly. "Captain," he said, "this passport has been given to me as evidence of

A cabildo

my official character. It is necessary for my personal secur-
ity, and I will not give it up."

Catherwood, who had been quietly watching, now
stepped forward and reminded the captain of the laws of
nations. "I should like to warn you," he said, "that ambas-
sadors have very special rights. I trust, sir, that you would
not wish to bring upon yourself the vengeance of the government *del Norte*."

There was no reply. Stephens repeated that he would
not surrender his passport. Rather than that, he said, he
would return the way he had come.

"You will not go anywhere," said the captain. "You will
stay here and give me your passport."

Stephens was now at the end of his patience.

"Finding arguments and remonstrances of no use," he
wrote, "I placed the paper inside my vest, buttoned my
coat tight across my breast, and told him he must get it by
force, to which the officer, with a gleam of satisfaction
crossing his villainous face, responded that he would. I
added, however, that whatever the immediate result, ultimately such action would be fatal to them, but he answered,
with a sneer, that they would run the risk.

"During all this time, the band of cowardly ruffians
stood with their hands on their swords and machetes, and
two assassin-looking scoundrels sat on a bench with muskets against their shoulders, the muzzles pointed within
three feet of my breast. If we had been longer in the country we should have been more alarmed, but as yet we did
not know the sanguinary character of the people, and the
whole proceeding was so outrageous and insulting that it
roused our indignation more than our fears.

"Augustin, having previously suffered a cut on the head
from a machete, was always bellicose, and he begged me
in French to give the order to fire, claiming that one round
would scatter them all. . . . If the young man himself had

laid his hands upon me, I think I should have knocked him down at least, but, most fortunately, before he had time to give his order a man wearing a glazed hat and roundabout jacket entered and asked to see the passport. I was determined not to trust it out of my hands, and held it up before a blazing pine stick while, at Mr. Catherwood's request, he read it aloud."

Hearing the passport read aloud had a visible effect on the soldiers, who decided not to take it by force. But the captain restated the order that Stephens and his party remain in the village.

Stephens had not by any means exhausted his bag of diplomatic tricks. He now demanded that a letter be taken immediately to the commanding general of the province in which they were traveling. The officers refused, but when Stephens offered to pay the expense of sending the courier, they changed their minds.

Taking his pen, Stephens wrote rapidly, explaining their arrest and imprisonment and the refusal of the *alcalde* or the soldiers to accept his official passport. He demanded to be set free and allowed to proceed unharmed.

When the letter was finished and sealed, the captain took it and, stationing twelve men with swords, muskets, and machetes at the entrance, went out of the *cabildo*. Locking the door, he warned the *alcalde*: "If they escape during the night—your head will answer for it!"

"The excitement over," Stephens wrote, "Mr. Catherwood and I were exhausted. What a beautiful beginning to our travels—only a month from home and here we were in the hands of men who would have been turned out of any decent state prison lest they contaminate the other boarders. A peep at our beautiful keepers did nothing to reassure us. They were sitting under the shed directly before the door, and smoking cigars around a fire, their arms in reach. Their whole stock of wearing apparel was not worth a pair of old boots, and with their rags, their arms, and their dark faces reddened by the firelight, their appearance was ferocious; if we attempted to escape, they would have been glad, doubtless, of the excuse for murder."

Stephens fastened the door inside, as a precautionary measure. Then the weary travelers crawled into their hammocks.

Quiet returned. The silence contrasted remarkably with all the noise and argument that had just transpired. Now it seemed as if their troubles were far away, that they were deep in a wilderness where the silence was rarely or never broken by sounds of human warfare.

Minutes passed and became hours . . . one . . . two . . . three.

The lock rattled and broke. The door burst open. By eerie light of blazing sticks, the motley band poured into the room again—swords, muskets, machetes, and all.

Stephens and Catherwood leaped to their feet. Without ceremony, they were handed back the letter to the general and told that they could proceed undisturbed. With that, the captain and his band turned and left.

Puzzled and relieved, Stephens and Catherwood watched the men depart. What lay behind it all, they knew not. Nor did they care to call the captain back for an explanation.

With a cup of chocolate, they celebrated their release, and not long after, as dawn came to the deserted village, they moved out onto the trail.

You cannot be in Guatemala long before hearing of ruined temples and buried cities. The irony of it is that here in the savage jungles of Central America the very thought of cities and temples seemed absurd. A highly developed race of people building giant monuments in this hot, humid, impenetrable forest? It didn't make sense. In Egypt, yes. Desert climates are wonderfully dry and healthful. The same could be said of Athens, and Rome, and the Arabian (now Jordanian) city of Petra, cut in solid stone, where Stephens had been in 1836. On the same trip he had climbed Mount Sinai, in what is now Egypt, sailed up the Nile, strolled through the ruins of Thebes by moonlight, and explored the temples of Amun at Luxor. A civilization could flourish in that exhilarating climate—and did.

But in the United States of Central America, with all its humidity, its mosquitoes, its diseases, one could expect only huts of mud and simple Indian villages. Temples? Statues? Monuments engraved with sculpture? Impossible!

Yet stories of Copán, the legendary ruined city in the mountains of Honduras, persisted, and at this moment only a single question remained in Stephens' mind. Should he go?

It was true that they had intended to explore as many ruins as they could on their trip, but he had to consider two things—one, the state of turmoil the country was in, and two, his special mission for President Van Buren. The mission had to come first; as a presidential emissary he must carry out his orders regardless of war or ancient ruins. He saw no compromise in that.

On the other hand, neither did he see any reason why he had to proceed immediately to Guatemala City. In all probability, the war would still be raging when he got there two or more weeks from now; the government for which he was searching would still be in whatever condition it was in now. Van Buren was eager to know what was happening in Central America—with all its uprisings and intrigues—but the President could wait a little.

And besides, as a matter of principle, Stephens figured he ought to learn more about the country before he arrived in Guatemala City. At least he could then talk intelligently about it.

And so they turned toward Honduras. Destination: Copán. (See map in Chapter 4.)

Rising early each day, before the morning fog had lifted

from the river bottoms, they proceeded into a broken, mountainous country. It was a land much drier and less jungle-like than that at the edge of the Motagua River, which by now they had left far behind.

Always in their ears, morning to night, was the ringing clip-clop of the mules' hoofs. It became a kind of drumbeat of the trail, accompanied by the music of jangling cups and forks and spoons in the packs. More delicate were the chronometer, (a clock-like instrument for measuring time), the sextant (with which to determine their geographical position), and a thermometer and telescope.

They were now going farther into the mountains with each step of the mules, with each passing hour. About all they knew was that the mysterious city of Copán (if it existed at all) lay somewhere beyond the border.

They came to lonely, isolated villages, each with its ruined church, its plaza shaded by palm trees, its fountain or spring attended by village women filling their water jars. At one place they saw hundreds of soldiers drawn up for a parade. Soldiers indeed! They were more like bandits than soldiers, Stephens thought. Perhaps they were both.

Time meant nothing here. Time was measured by crossings of rugged mountain ranges, one after another, or of jungles and tortuous canyons. Time meant even less when they came to the Copán River, a broad, clear stream that drained a region of richly wooded peaks. Soon they were in the State of Honduras. Now, for Stephens, time stood still.

The arrival of the strangers in the village of Copán, which consisted of a half-dozen huts thatched with corn leaves, created a sensation. The Indians gathered to watch, but, when asked where the ancient ruins were, replied that they did not know. With difficulty Stephens finally found a villager who knew where the ruins were and could guide him to them.

Next morning the party set out on the final leg of its

journey. For a while the caravan's way led past primitive cornfields. As he watched the Indians caring for their crops, Stephens wondered where the earliest of their ancestors had come from. Various theories on this subject could be found in books, one being that the Indians were remnants of the great flood in the days of Noah. Some historians felt that people as wild and savage as these could hardly be related to the ones who had built the fabled cities hidden in the forest.

But Stephens remembered glowing accounts of the Aztec Indians, whom Cortéz had conquered in Mexico more than 300 years before. Would that he and Catherwood could find a group of temples similar to those over which the Aztec chieftain Montezuma had ruled! If there were any ruins older than that (Montezuma ruled in the early 1500's), historians did not know about them. As one said: "There is not, in all the extent of that vast empire, a single monument or vestige of any building more ancient than the Conquest."

And how wrong he was! There were, in fact, three main groups of Indians in Central and South America: the Incas, Aztecs, and Mayas. The Incas, native to the Andes, occupied lands far south of here, from Colombia down into Argentina. They lived on desert coasts, in jungles, and on mountain peaks. By conquering and subjecting pre-Inca civilizations to theirs, they skillfully wove together one elongated empire connected by over 2,500 miles of roads.

Their decline and fall began in 1532 when Spaniards under Francisco Pizarro moved into their land. Today some five million descendants of the Incas still remain in the Andes highlands.

The Aztecs, on the other hand, did not settle as far south as South America. They came to the area around the lakes of Anáhuac (where Mexico City stands today) in A.D. 1168, emigrating from raw, cold zones to the north. They moved first onto rocky islets in Lake Texcoco, and within a few hundred years had built a great city-state, sprawling over an area of 1,500 square miles. Under Montezuma, this city became in many ways more advanced than comparable European cities of its time. The Aztecs were conquered by Cortéz in 1521, and today their descendants still live in Mexico.

The third great group were the Mayas. Christopher Columbus was the first European to see them. Off the coast of Honduras he encountered a dugout bearing twenty-five Indians. They came, he said, from a province called "Maian." In their heyday, the Mayas occupied large portions of what are now Honduras, Guatemala, and Yucatán—the eastern peninsula of Mexico. When Stephens rode his mule into the highlands of Central America, the descendants of the Mayas still lived there—as they do today.

But it was not modern Mayas he sought. It was the temples built by their ancestors.

Turning off the main path, the little party of explorers, with its Maya guide, soon came to a wood so thick that none could ride through. Dismounting, they tied their mules to trees and entered the forest, following the Indian guide who cleared their way with a sharp machete. It was a dark forest. The gloom of it matched Stephens' gloom at the slim chance of finding any ruined cities so far back in the jungle. Humboldt hadn't. The German naturalist Alexander von Humboldt, then of world renown and a hero of Stephens, had seen and written about the ruins of Mexico, but had apparently never visited, or even heard of, any others.

Thus Stephens made his way through the jungle with a sense of curiosity rather than certainty about what they would find. As he said, he had more hope than expectation of coming upon prehistoric wonders.

Suddenly they were at the bank of the river, and the

The wall at Copán

guide was pointing across to the other side. They looked up
and saw a wall, an incredibly old stone wall, overgrown
with trees and vines. In most places, Stephens calculated,
the wall was a hundred feet high; in others it had fallen
into ruin.

All doubt vanished as if it had been a cloud. They had
had but a glimpse, yet what they had seen was a *wall*. That
was enough!

They returned to their mules, mounted, and forded the
stream as rapidly as the mules would carry them. Presently
they were standing at the base of the wall. Here it became
obvious that the stones had been carefully cut and well laid
and, despite the encroaching vegetation, were fairly well
preserved.

After climbing up on a terrace, they made their way
through woods that hid the ruins and soon came upon a
stone column about three feet square and fourteen feet

Stone idol B at Copán

*Artist's drawing of Copán as it must
have looked when occupied by the Mayas*

high, more than twice Stephens' own height. His eyes, and
Catherwood's too, must have opened wide with amazement.
The column, or *stela,* was sculptured deeply on all sides,
from top to bottom, with strange symbols and figures of
men richly dressed.

"The sight of this unexpected monument," Stephens was
to write, "put at rest once and forever all uncertainty in our
minds as to the character of American antiquities, and gave
us the assurance that the objects we were in search of
were not only interesting as the remains of an unknown
people, but were works of art as well, proving, like newly
discovered historical records, that the people who once
occupied the American continents were not savages."

3

A BURIED CITY

O O O

HOWLING, swinging through the trees, breaking off branches, the monkeys clambered about in agitation as the intruders invaded their domain. In groups of forty or fifty at a time they leaped among the treetops, sailing from branch to branch, creating the sound of a windstorm swirling through the forest.

Colorful motmot birds, with their long tail feathers, swooped and chattered among the trees. Iguana lizards, three feet long and formidable-looking, leaped down the trunks and onto the slopes. Insects dipped and zoomed from sunlight into gloom, where only patches of ground were illuminated beneath the canopy of leaves.

There in the shadows Stephens and Catherwood peered among the tangled roots of trees, straining to make out the sculptured rows of figures, death's heads, and undecipherable inscriptions. It seemed to Stephens as if the mocking monkeys and motmots were long-lost ghosts of the builders of this city—laughing at the perplexity of the explorers.

Crossing a terrace overgrown with trees, Stephens ordered the Indians, with their machetes, to clear away the growth. When this was done, they looked across an open square with steps on all sides. "Almost as perfect as those of a Roman amphitheater!" Stephens whispered.

The steps were highly ornamented, and on one side about halfway up was a colossal head. They climbed the steps and reached a high terrace overlooking the river.

"We sat down on the very edge of the wall," wrote Stephens, "and strove in vain to penetrate the mystery by which we were surrounded. Who were the people that built this city? In the ruined cities of Egypt, even in the long-lost Petra, the stranger knows the story of the people whose vestiges he finds around him. America, say historians, was peopled by savages; but savages never reared these structures, savages never carved these stones. When we asked the Indians who had made them, their dull answer was *'Quién sabe?'* ['Who knows?']. . . .

"Architecture, sculpture, and painting, all the arts which embellish life, had flourished in this overgrown forest; orators, warriors, and statesmen, beauty, ambition, and glory had lived and passed away. . . .

"The city was desolate. . . . It lay before us like a shattered bark in the midst of the ocean, her masts gone, her name effaced, her crew perished, and none to tell whence she came, to whom she belonged, how long on her voyage, or what caused her destruction. . . . The place where we were sitting, was it a citadel from which an unknown people had sounded the trumpet of war? Or a temple for the worship of the God of peace? Or did the inhabitants worship idols made with their own hands and offer sacrifices on the stones before them?"

The mystery swept over Stephens with what he called an intense, almost wild interest. He wanted to start at once to explore the whole city, although he could see that whatever he did would not be simple. It had been so easy to wander through Egyptian ruins. But Maya ruins were densely covered with forest, the very stones being split by roots relentlessly growing . . . growing . . . growing.

Wearily the little party returned to the foot of the wall, bathed in the river, and retired for the night.

The hut that was to be their home while exploring Copán stood at the edge of a clearing where the Indians had planted corn and tobacco. The hut was sixteen feet square, with a peaked thatch roof supported by upright

The hut at Copán

poles. With only a primitive bed, a stone roller for mashing corn, and an earthen griddle for making corn cakes called *tortillas* it wasn't much of a home. But it was near the ruins, and that's what counted.

A flash of lightning blinded them, and then they heard an ominous rumble. The natural elements that would plague them over and over burst across the mountains. Stephens had a definite opinion of these torments:

"The clouds became blacker than ever; on the left was a range of naked mountains and the old stone quarries of Copán, along which the thunder rolled fearfully while the lightning wrote angry inscriptions on its sides. An English tourist in the United States once admitted the superiority of our thunder and lightning. Although I am pertinacious on all points of national honor, I concede this claim in favor of the tropics. The rain fell as if floodgates had been opened from above. . . ."

Each day, at daylight, clouds hung over the forest, but as the sun rose they cleared away. Workmen arrived at the hut and then, over muddy ground, beneath dripping trees, made their way to the ruins to clear and excavate them.

An immense task it was! Who knew how many ruins there were or how far back among the trees they extended? Parts of the growth that covered the ruins were so heavy no one could walk through it—or even see through it. If they could cut down the forest and burn the trees, the nature of this ruined city would be revealed. But they had neither men.enough nor time enough to cut all the trees down, and the forest was too wet to burn.

At least they could examine some of the sculptured columns closely, and Catherwood could draw them. But drawing in a studio and drawing among the ruins of Copán were entirely different. In the darkness beneath the foliage it would have required magic vision to see the extremely complicated carvings, much less copy them. The forest would have to be cut away to expose the ruins to sunlight.

But the only cutting tools the Indians had were machetes—excellent against vines and shrubs but poor against trees. Besides, the Indians appeared to Stephens to be the world's slowest workers, as if trying to see how few trees they could cut in a day. Nevertheless, he had no other help in cutting the forest—no lumberjacks, no axes, no saws—and he was determined to make do with what he had.

With the lowly machete, the slow-paced Indians finally cleared away one of the stone monuments, and Catherwood started to work.

Torture would be a better word. This was not nearly as easy as drawing pictures of ruins in Egypt and Jerusalem. Here, Catherwood had to stand with his feet in mud. Water dripped from the trees overhead. Mosquitoes swarmed into his eyes and ears and nose; they stung his hands so badly that he had to wear gloves. And all the time, his body ached with fever and rheumatism, probably aggravated by the dampness.

To make matters worse, the carvings on the ancient monuments were so strange and intricate that he had to copy them as if his eyes and brain were a *camera lucida,* an instrument which, through mirrors or prisms, conveyed the image of an object onto paper or canvas so that it could be traced exactly. And how does an artist make delicate drawings with gloved hands?

All these difficulties make the task seem impossible. And so it may have seemed to Catherwood at first. But as the days went by, as mosquitoes buzzed and trees dripped, he produced some strikingly detailed reproductions of the ancient monuments of Copán.

Meanwhile, the cutters and choppers kept ahead of Catherwood. In turn, Stephens kept ahead of *them*—measuring distances with a tape, calculating heights, taking notes, studying shapes and designs of half-hidden buildings. Wherever he could, he re-erected fallen monuments.

The greatest task, perhaps, was picking out specific objects for Catherwood to copy. There was so much!

Day after day they worked, steadily and often painfully, stopping only long enough to eat. Their meals, consisting of staples such as beans and beef, eggs, bread and milk, were prepared by Augustin from foods obtained in the village or at *haciendas* (farms) in the neighborhood.

When he had uncovered monuments enough to occupy Catherwood for a while, Stephens began a general survey of the ruins. He was no engineer, but you could not expect John Lloyd Stephens to wait until an engineer could be brought in from some distant city or country. Now was the time! Yet he was faced with almost total lack of information about the ruins of Copán.

Stephens had no way of estimating how old these ruins were, only that they were already objects of antiquity when

Tablet of hieroglyphics at Copán

the Spaniards conquered Mexico and Central America shortly after A.D. 1500.

There had been a report, about the year 1700, that certain of these buildings remained entire and were fairly
well preserved. They had been described by Francisco de
Fuentes y Guzmán, who wrote a history of Guatemala.
There was no other account of the ruins until the one by
a Colonel Galindo, in 1836, a few years prior to Stephens'
visit. The trouble was that all these accounts were incomplete. No plans or drawings had ever been published.

Feeling like a pioneer, Stephens came upon one after
another of the wonders of Copán. He discovered another
amphitheater and the ruin of a temple all but enveloped by
the tentacles of a strangler-fig tree. There were walls, terraces, staircases, and pyramids everywhere he looked, as
well as the fallen sides of what may once have been
gateways.

As he climbed among the ruins and through the en-
tangling trees, Stephens came upon large fragments of
sculpture, including beautifully fashioned heads that may
have represented chieftains. Some structures were adorned
with death's heads, or animals, or what appeared to be
priests. More often than not, he came to exquisite carvings
that meant absolutely nothing. They were hieroglyphic
writings, but unlike any he had seen.

Most wonderful of all were the monuments, the "idols"
as he called them. Nearly all were more than twice as tall
as he, each carved from a single block of stone. The sculpture, richly covering all four sides, was an intricate mixture
of human figures, symbols, and ornamental designs.

In the midst of the ruins he came to a curious stone that
looked like an altar, cut from a single block to a size of six
feet square and four feet high. On top were thirty-six
carved symbols which he presumed to be a description of
some event in the history of the Mayas. On each side were

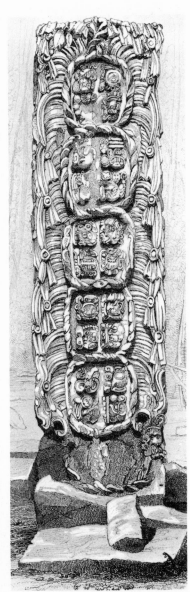

Stone idol Q at Copán: (left) front view; (right) back view

Stone altar at Copán: (top) south side; (bottom) east side

four seated men, dressed differently and wearing elaborate hats. He judged them to be warriors or chiefs assembled in conference. Each held an object, the use of which could only be guessed at.

Suddenly Stephens was struck with a peculiar fact: although he had imagined some of the carvings to represent warriors, there was really no solid evidence of war in the sculpture and works of art he had seen, or at least no violent battle scenes. Such things were prominent among the antiquities of other nations, but not here. These people had apparently been peaceable. Had they thus been easily conquered?

Sculptured heads, some fallen into the debris, the whole intertwined by roots of trees and covered with moss, seemed to be a legacy of Copán. Stephens was sure that other great discoveries lay in the giant mounds of rubble that he gazed at wistfully. If only he had a large, dependable crew of cutters and diggers, and plenty of time, Copán would yield up its secrets.

He found a pit five feet square and seventeen feet deep, at the bottom of which was an opening into a vault. An earlier explorer had found red earthenware pots in there, of which more than fifty held human bones. What manner of priests or chieftains had been laid to rest in such a place?

Cutting, digging, removing as much debris as possible, Stephens and his crew opened to view artistic workmanship of grace and beauty—or of such ugly and distorted figures as to inspire terror. One monument, nearly twelve feet high, had originally been painted red, for a little of the color remained. A figure on one side was of good workmanship, though parts had been worn and scarred by erosion. The back of the monument (see page 41) contained strange scenes as if from a nightmare.

Never before had he seen such designs, or ornaments, or contortions of human figures. He had no idea what the figures were supposed to be doing, or what the carved scenes were supposed to represent. The imagination, he said, was pained in gazing at them. Over all the ruins was a feeling of solemnity, even of superstition, which was the way the present-day Indians looked at them.

Howler monkeys stared down quizzically from the trees, adding to the air of solemnity, but in the afternoons they came "promenading" out among the treetops.

There were other visitors, too, which disturbed the careful measurements Stephens was trying to make and the drawings Catherwood was trying to finish. These were *garrapatas*—ticks. Both men tied their trousers tightly around their boots and buttoned their coats around their necks. It didn't work. The ticks got in, found their way beneath the clothes, and buried themselves in the flesh.

Mosquitoes never ceased, and everyone had to watch for scorpions with which the ruins abounded. Worse yet, in their hut at night, exhausted after a day's work, the

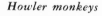

Howler monkeys

explorers had to shield themselves from hordes of fleas.

This was bad enough, but then the food from nearby farms and villages became much harder to get, until eventually Stephens and his party were reduced to eating little more than *tortillas.*

Yet none of this deterred the author or the artist. They proceeded as if each day would be their last, trying to do as much as they could before they had to leave. It looked as if the muddy trip over Mico Mountain would prove to have been worth every step.

Since Stephens' visit, the ruins of Copán have been extensively, though not entirely, explored, and many of the buildings have been restored. Archeologists estimate that Copán reached its peak of architecture and sculpture around the year A.D. 790, and that some of the carved stelae may have been erected as early as A.D. 465.

Altogether, the ruins cover seventy-five acres, the equivalent of fifty-six modern football fields, and because of additions made by the Mayas, the site has terraces, temples, pyramids, and plazas in majestic array.

The main plaza is surrounded by tiers of seats, something like a present-day football field. But this field had neither goalposts nor ball players. The nine stelae standing in it, plus the elaborately carved altars, testify that rather than games, important ceremonies must have been held here. The people of Copán were not without games however; a small court nearby has been identified as a ball court.

The Mayas had hard rubber balls to play with, and their ball game was called *pok-a-tok.* Religious rituals may have been performed before a game, but the game itself, as far as is known, was for sport. With the Mayas, as with present-day Americans, says one archeologist, games were sometimes given more consideration than serious matters.

Nearby is the Court of the Hieroglyphic Stairway, which

was so deeply buried by debris that Stephens saw little of it. Now restored, this wide stairway of sixty-two steps is an object of great artistic value. Carved in the steps are nearly 2,000 separate glyphs, or characters, the longest inscription thus far discovered in Maya ruins.

In another plaza a short distance away lies the Jaguar Stairway, with standing stone jaguars whose bodies were once adorned with polished black obsidian (volcanic glass) to represent spots.

Many of the archeological discoveries at Copán were made by the Carnegie Institution of Washington, D.C., which has been working at Copán, in cooperation with the government of Honduras, since 1935. Findings from these excavations and studies have encouraged the belief that Copán was a center of scientific learning, especially astronomy. One temple was dedicated to the planet Venus, another to a specific discovery—the exact length of intervals between solar eclipses.

Whoever the astronomers were at Copán, their calculations of eclipse periods as well as of the length of the solar year were more accurate than elsewhere in the Maya empire. One can well imagine that an eclipse of something as sacred and life-giving as the sun must have been regarded by the superstitious Mayas as a portent of calamity. The sun, being dimmed, was obviously under attack. Hence the priests desired to know when the next eclipse was due so that they could prepare their people for disaster. What if the sun *stayed* eclipsed? Apparently the Mayas never deduced that the earth revolved around the sun.

Thus we see that in the Honduras uplands there was once a center of science, art, and architecture. Stephens had an inkling of all this, especially after he had cleared away part of the covering bushes and trees. And Catherwood's detailed drawings first showed the world how advanced the Maya civilization had become, at least in art.

Hieroglyphic stairway at Copán

4

HIGH COUNTRY
OOOO

"IT is impossible to describe the interest with which I explored these ruins. The ground was entirely new; there were no guidebooks or guides; the whole was a virgin soil. We could not see ten yards before us, and never knew what we should stumble upon next. . . .

"I leaned over with breathless anxiety while the Indians worked, and an eye, an ear, a foot, or a hand was disentombed; and when the machete rang against the chiseled stone, I pushed the Indians away and cleared out the loose earth with my hands. The beauty of the sculpture, the solemn stillness of the woods disturbed only by the scrambling of monkeys and the chattering of parrots, the desolation of the city, and the mystery that hung over it, all created an interest higher, if possible, than I had ever felt among the ruins of the Old World."

Measuring, cutting, clearing paths from ruin to ruin and monument to monument, Stephens opened to the tropic sun as many of the buried objects as he could. With an eagerness born of travel among ancient cities he reported to the patient Catherwood, now wearing waterproof boots and standing on a piece of oiled canvas that was regularly used for covering their luggage on the road, that there were ruins galore to be copied.

The sun now seemed to fall just right to highlight the sculptured monuments and make them easy for Catherwood to draw. Even so, the crowded designs, the delicate lines, partly worn away, the unfamiliar faces of the Indians, and strange gyrations of their bodies gave him trouble.

To copy perfectly was Catherwood's goal. If he could do that, then each of his original drawings could later be reproduced by engravers and published as a faithful likeness of the object itself. Any error here would be magnified in the printing process—so there must be no errors. Despite the mosquitoes, despite the ticks, despite the fleas and the steady diet of *tortillas*—he had to be absolutely accurate.

The more they saw, the more they wondered about the people who carved these monuments and built the buildings. No one could tell by merely looking at the ruins how long ago they had been built, or how long ago the people had lived and worked and died.

"In regard to the age of this desolate city," Stephens wrote, "I shall not at present offer any conjecture. Some idea might perhaps be formed from the accumulations of earth and the gigantic trees growing on the top of the ruined structures, but it would be uncertain and unsatisfactory. Nor shall I at this moment offer any conjecture in regard

A self-portrait of Catherwood at work. He is holding measuring tape (rear right) while Stephens (at left) carries it

to the people who built it; or to the time when or the means by which it was depopulated to become a desolation and ruin; or as to whether it fell by the sword, or famine, or pestilence.

"The trees which shroud it may have sprung from the blood of its slaughtered inhabitants; they may have perished howling with hunger; or pestilence, like the cholera, may have piled its streets with the dead and driven forever the feeble remnants from their homes. . . .

"One thing I believe: its history is graven on its monuments."

In Stephens' day, there was no clear notion as to the origin of North American Indians. Archeologists would later discover evidence to suggest that the earliest people came to to this hemisphere from Asia, by way of Alaska, more than ten thousand years ago. With the passage of time, more Indians came and their descendants continued toward the southern tip of South America. Some Indians wandered and hunted. Some learned to farm, then settled down to raise crops, to think, to build cities, and to make weapons, jewelry, and other objects. Some would be called Aztecs, some Incas, some Mayas.

It was while he was deep in the exploration of Copán that Stephens remembered, perhaps a trifle painfully, the primary purpose of his mission to Central America. He had, after all, been sent here by the President of the United States to find whatever government existed. Instead of seeking ruins, he should be seeking public officials.

He had never expected, when they turned off the main road to Guatemala City in search of Copán, that they would be gone more than two or three days. That was two weeks ago. Now he knew that he had to be on his way. If he didn't, his mission could fail entirely. If civil war broke out, he and Catherwood might be expelled from the country before their journey had scarcely begun.

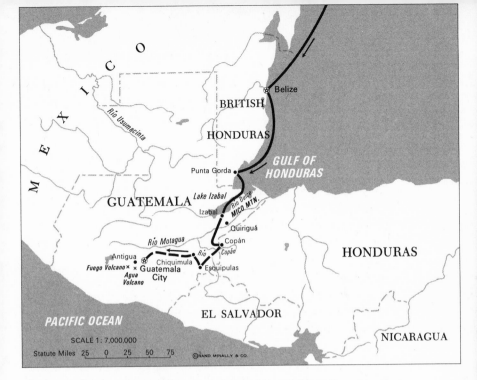

Routes of Stephens and Catherwood from New York to the ruins of Copán, in Honduras; and from Copán to Guatemala City, in 1839

Stephens had cleared away enough of the ruins to keep Catherwood busy for a month. Why couldn't Catherwood stay and finish the drawings? The two of them could then meet in Guatemala City.

The more they thought about it, the more they liked the idea. They would be able to keep their two jobs going at once. So be it. Stephens called his men, packed up and saddled his mule, and Catherwood accompanied him to the edge of the woods to say good-by.

Then the red-haired New Yorker mounted and rode out of Copán.

He must have stopped across the river for one last look at the wall of the ruined city. "Here, as the sculptor worked," he wrote, "he turned to the theatre of his glory, as the Greek did to the Acropolis of Athens, and dreamed of immortal fame. Little did he imagine that the time would come when his works would perish, his race be extinct, his city a desolation and the abode of reptiles for strangers to gaze at and wonder by what race it had once been inhabited."

The caravan that went up the mountain trail that day consisted of Stephens, Augustin, a muleteer, and seven mules. They must have seemed a funny sight to the Indians of the highlands. Their luggage was wrapped in cowhides. Cups and pans and forks clanked in packs on the sides of the mules. The muleteer usually cursed in a loud voice. And when a mule broke loose and ran away, or floundered in a ravine, they all went chasing after it in high good humor or with shouts of exasperation.

Over the mountains and through the wilderness they rode—out of Honduras and back into Guatemala. Soon they came to the village of Esquipulas, where they heard exactly what Stephens did not want to hear: trouble lay ahead.

"There is danger, *Señor*," he was told. "Troops under General Carrera guard the roads to Guatemala City."

"But we have a passport," Stephens protested.

"*Si, Señor*," came the reply, "but these are Indian troops. They do not read English. They do not read Spanish. Ha! They do not read!"

Due to these conditions of uncertainty they could now expect murder and robbery to be commonplace in the country. In fact, as Stephens learned later, plans had been made to waylay him in the mountains. Had he not crossed in the morning (robberies were usually committed in the afternoon, he said) he might have been robbed and killed. But at the time of his trip he was unaware of any specific danger to himself. What he did hear was that two Englishmen had been arrested in Honduras and their muleteers and servants murdered. How long would Catherwood be safe?

Esquipulas as it is today (Basilica in background)

It was no place for the timid! One night the *alcalde* of a village in which Stephens was staying came to inform him that robbers were at that very moment after him. Leaping up, swords and guns in their hands, Stephens and his men sallied into the darkness. What followed was a confused pursuit out of the village and into the mountains, but nothing came of the affair. Stephens returned to the village muttering: "I am heartily sick of the country and its petty alarms."

The coming of day erased his gloom. In crystal air and bright sunshine they continued on their way past cultivated fields of indigo, sugar cane, and corn, into wild and scenic ravines, and up rugged mountain slopes that gave them splendid views of the country. He was reminded of parts of Switzerland that he had seen.

The day after that they rose still higher on the plateau and finally arrived at their destination. "Late in the afternoon"—Stephens was eloquent in describing the scene—"as I was ascending a small eminence, two immense volcanoes stood up before me, seeming to scorn the earth and towering to the heavens. They were the great volcanoes of Agua and Fuego, forty miles distant, and nearly fifteen thousand feet high, wonderfully grand and beautiful.

"In a few moments the great plain of Guatemala appeared in view, surrounded by mountains; in its center was the city, a mere speck on the vast expanse, with churches and convents, and numerous turrets, cupolas, and steeples, still as if the spirit of peace rested upon it. . . .

"I dismounted and tied my mule. As yet the sun lighted up the roofs and domes of the city, giving a reflection so dazzling that I could only look at them by stealth. By degrees its disk touched the top of the Volcán de Agua; slowly the whole orb sank behind it, illuminating the background with an atmosphere fiery red. A rich golden cloud rolled up its side and rested on the top and, while I gazed, the golden hues disappeared and the glory . . . was gone."

Basilica in marketplace at Esquipulas today

5

GUATEMALA

[========]

THE United States of Central America had been established in 1823, two years after all the Central American countries, and Mexico, had torn off the yoke of Spanish rule and declared themselves independent. All this must have intrigued young Stephens, who had then been seventeen years of age, attending law school in Connecticut. After all, the United States of America had torn off a yoke of its own— British rule—not fifty years before. Now here was a neighboring nation doing the same.

But would the new republic last? States of Central America were not as closely knit as states of the U.S.A. Few people could read or write. Most were Indian, accustomed to fending for themselves and to solving their problems individually or tribally. Few, if any, had experience in communal affairs. Each tribe lived in a world of its own, far back in the hills, or down in the depths of the jungle, and some provinces were separated by mountain ranges.

Each state—Guatemala, Honduras, Costa Rica, Nicaragua, and El Salvador—had a separate history and differed in customs and outlook from the others. There were few roads, little money, and not much of an army.

All things considered, about all anyone could expect was that the new republic would falter and fall apart. There was not much to hold it together. The surprise was that it had been put together in the first place—even temporarily.

Very soon, civil war had broken out. The president, Manuel José Arce, was forced to resign, and his place was taken by a Honduran named Francisco Morazán, then thirty

years old. Morazán, immensely popular, did what he could
to pull the people together and reform the ways of the
wicked, but it was no use.

An epidemic of cholera worsened the situation, and before long the Indians rose in revolt. Under twenty-three-
year-old Rafael Carrera, they went on a wild rampage.

Bells sounded the alarm. Citizens fled into houses and
courtyards where they frantically slammed and bolted the
doors. Window shutters were closed and tightly snapped
into place.

Sure enough, the rebel army was approaching. But what
an army! Robbers, murderers, outlaws—half-naked Indians
so fresh from the hills that they had never seen a city before.

In a vast horde they came, twelve thousand of them, a
disorderly crowd led by the young half-breed, Carrera, on
horseback. They were armed with the strangest assortment
of weapons that had ever menaced the citizens of Guatemala City. Whoever dared to peer out the window saw
Indians carrying knives, machetes, clubs, sticks, rusty muskets, and old pistols—anything with which they could fight.

"Viva la religión!" the Indians shouted. "Muerte a los
extranjeros!" ("Long live religion! Death to foreigners!")

Fear gripped the city as Carrera and his ragged mob
moved in. Men of the much-too-small army garrison, whose
job it was to defend the city, either fled or laid down their
arms in surrender.

Without a fight, the mass of unruly invaders flooded into
town. They choked the streets, entered the churches, attacked houses, murdered the vice-president, and generally
sacked the city. Carrera was finally paid thousands of
dollars to take his army away. And the remaining authorities gave him and his band a thousand muskets.

Stephens had heard of Carrera, and of this first assault
on Guatemala City. It had happened the year before his

arrival and was still fresh in the minds of the people. Hearing about it reminded him of the invasion of Rome. Not since then, thought Stephens, had a civilized city been overwhelmed with such a flood of barbarians.

The sacking of Guatemala City was the beginning of Carrera's bloodstained road to power. He quickly put those thousand muskets to use. Battles and skirmishes raged. Provinces began to secede from the Union and set themselves up as independent nations, forcing Morazán into exile. When that happened, Carrera established himself as ruler of Guatemala.

Small wonder that the President of the United States of America had been puzzled by what was going on. The situation was so confused that not even the people of Central America knew what kind of a government they had—if they had one.

This was why President Van Buren had sent John Lloyd Stephens to this land of turmoil. He hoped that Stephens could bring back news of

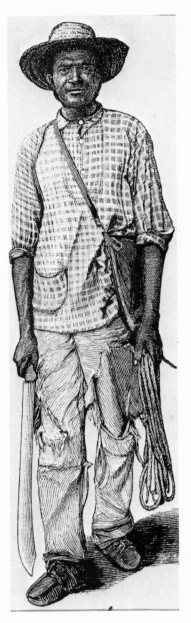

Indian with machete

what was happening. Stephens hoped so, too—if he could get out alive!

His arrival in Guatemala City, under the circumstances, was unceremonious—hardly befitting a personal emissary of the President *del Norte!* His mule had broken its bridle and Stephens was forced to lead the animal through the streets instead of riding in dignity upon it.

Not knowing where else to go, he got an Indian to guide them to the home of the British Vice-Consul.

"How did you get here?" asked the Consul. "I would have opened the door for you sooner, but today the soldiers mutinied for want of pay and have threatened to sack the city."

"We had no trouble here," Stephens replied, "but we were arrested and detained in a village toward the coast."

"Well, you are fortunate. The citizens are greatly alarmed. I used to fly a flag here, but on their last entry these stupid soldiers—mind you, they are Indians, and the worst of the lot—fired on the flag, calling it a *bandera de guerra.*"

"A war flag? Don't they know—"

"They are mostly from the villages—insolent, ignorant. . . . A few days ago I had my hat knocked off by a sentinel because I did not raise it in passing. I assure you that my complaint upon this is before the government." The Consul shook his head. "It is a pity. Guatemala was once the jewel of Spanish America. Now see what's done to it. . . ."

"Where is the government of the United States of Central America? Where is Morazán?"

The Vice-Consul smiled wryly. "*Quién sabe?* Three states have seceded from the central government. The rest are held together God knows how. Guatemala has declared itself free. The present government has been in power for six months— rather surprised, I think, at its own success."

"And Carrera?"

"He flutters between arrogance and brutality on the one hand and fear on the other. He is unpredictable. Who knows what he will do next?"

"Well," said Stephens, "I must see him."

"Take care," the Vice-Consul warned. "You Americans have no Consul here, you know. The only American inhabitant of Guatemala City is Mr. Hall, the former Consul. And mark you—do not wander in the streets at night."

Stephens retired in what was to him great luxury: it was the first time since he had left the ship—almost two months earlier—that he had had a good bed and clean sheets.

Next morning he breathed the pure and invigorating air of Guatemala City. At 4,850 feet above the sea, it was in the midst of a land of eternal spring, cool, refreshing, restful.

The city itself had been founded in 1776, the same year that the United States of America was born. Its graceful churches, colorful and elegantly ornamented, would have made tourists wide-eyed—had there been any tourists. Nearly every house, it seemed, had an enclosed, spacious garden, or at least a central court. The houses had massive doors with sturdy latches; the windows, iron balconies.

Stephens noticed that the houses were low, one-storied, strongly constructed to withstand movements of the ground. You could not forget that this was earthquake country. Not many years before, an earthquake had struck the former capital of Antigua, a picturesque city twenty-five miles away, at the foot of towering volcanoes. Antigua had been so badly shattered that the Spanish authorities had moved the capital to Guatemala City.

In the center of the city, then, as now, was the plaza, and in this stood a large stone fountain, surrounded, from time to time, by an open-air market. Several buildings faced the plaza, including the city hall with offices of the chief officials. There were also a school and a cathedral.

"I have seldom been more favorably impressed with the first appearance of any city," Stephens wrote in his journal, "and the only thing that pained me in a two hours' stroll through the streets was the sight of Carrera's ragged and insolent-looking soldiers; my first thought was that in any city in Europe or the United States the citizens, instead of submitting to be lorded over by such barbarians, would rise en masse and pitch them out of the gates."

And yet, it was not entirely a city of fear. From the very moment he arrived, Stephens was struck with the religious character of the people of Guatemala City.

He saw religious processions in which the streets were strewn with pine needles and graced with colorful, flower-covered arches. He walked under brilliant red-silk decorations that fluttered from windows and balconies.

It seemed as if the Catholics, their faith so evident everywhere in Central America, had erected beautifully ornamented churches and convents in every village and city. And it seemed as if they were forever holding processions or sponsoring celebrations. Church bells rang. Rockets

Central Square, Guatemala City, as it is today

soared into the air. Firecrackers were set off on the steps of churches. Sometimes frames of fireworks thirty feet high were ignited. People gathered in crowds to watch the dazzling exhibitions. Odors of gunpowder mingled with odors of incense. Music welled up in the background, and low humming and the singing of chants could be heard.

Stephens now and then went inside one of the churches. He saw kneeling women with black *mantillas* pulled over their heads and held together under the chin. Never, he thought, had he seen a more beautiful spectacle than these women, their heads held high and proudly, their faces aglow with enthusiasm for their religion.

"All day I had felt particularly the influence of the beautiful climate," wrote Stephens, "the mere breathing of the air was a luxury. And the evening was worthy of such a day; the moonbeams were lighting up the facade of the venerable church, showing in sadness a rent made by an earthquake from top to bottom. As we walked home, the streets were lighted with a brilliancy almost unearthly; and the ladies, proud of their moonlight, almost persuaded me that it was a land to love."

The gaiety of Guatemala City was pleasant—and strangely out of place—in a country so upset, but Stephens knew that the mere enjoying of it was not the way to fulfill his mission. He had been sent to find the government of the United States of Central America. Guatemala had seceded from that body, and so could not be said to represent it. Who did? Where was the central government?

The British Vice-Consul had told him he did not know where it was.

Yet rumors persisted about Morazán, the President. Would he come back to wrest Guatemala from Carrera and reunite the Union? The people trembled at such a thought. The streets would run with blood if Morazán returned.

Faced with all this, Stephens began to work out his problem. He learned that if there *was* a federation, the capital might be in El Salvador, a tiny country adjoining Guatemala on the south.

And if it were. . . . The words of his instructions came back to him: "You are to make a diligent search. . . ."

A diligent search! Despite the warfare, the lack of information, the dangers, he could not surrender. He, an appointed representative of the President of the United States of America, a diplomat, an envoy, could only go forward as long as there remained alive the slightest chance of finding what he came to find.

So, in the end, there was really no choice.

Having decided to proceed on his journey, and having made an appointment to pay an official visit to Carrera, Stephens got busy. He arranged for Catherwood to be properly guided, and his equipment transported, from Copán, where the drawings would soon be finished.

Well aware of troubles ahead, Stephens asked for help from key officials and heads of the church. They gave him letters that would identify him and his party, thus getting them out of trouble—if necessary.

The most important visit, of course, was to Carrera, whose name he had heard evoked in terms of terror or of loathing. Carrera was master of Guatemala, a hero to the rebels who had overthrown the government and withdrawn from the United States of Central America. He was a hero to the church as well, because of his battle cry of *"Viva la religión!"*

But Stephens had not forgotten the other half of that battle cry. "Death to foreigners!" He had heard it from the lips of armed, ragged, ill-bred rebels. A city with such a slogan, and where musket shots exploded night and day, seemed hardly a place for strangers. And with ragged soldiers prowling the countryside, Stephens knew perfectly

Carrera portrait and signature

well that he needed tangible proof of Carrera's friendship.

The hour approached for their appointed meeting. Carrera, they told him, was impressed with what they called "external show," and what others might term "pomp and circumstance." Good enough. Like every foreign-service officer, Stephens had come prepared. He got out his diplomatic coat, with all its glittering buttons, and donned it as if he, too, were an eminent leader.

Upon his arrival at the small and unpretentious house where Carrera happened to be staying, Stephens was halted by sentinels. Nearby stood Carrera's personal bodyguard, men dressed in red jackets and plaid caps.

Stephens was led into the house and down a corridor lined with muskets that had been carefully cleaned and shined—obviously ready for use.

In a room next to the living room, Carrera sat at a table counting money. How young he looked! Stephens thought. The facial features and expression, the lack of beard, and the straight black hair, indicated the youthful leader's Indian origin. He was no more than five-and-a-half feet tall, and wore a black jacket with pantaloons.

Could this be the master of the country? Could this be he who last year had been a wanted man, as proclaimed by the posters?

NOTICE
The person or persons who may deliver the criminal Rafael Carrera, dead or alive (if he does not present himself voluntarily under the last pardon), shall receive a reward of fifteen hundred dollars and two *caballerías* of land, and pardon for any crime he has committed.

The General-in-Chief,
J. N. Carvallo

Guatemala, July 20, 1838

Now Carrera, and not Morazán, ruled. Next week, or next year, who could tell?

There were other persons in the room. As soon as Carrera saw Stephens, he pushed aside his money, rose, and "probably out of respect to my coat," Stephens said, "received me with courtesy and gave me a chair at his side."

As he sat down, Stephens remarked upon Carrera's youth. Carrera was flattered, convinced apparently that he was an extraordinary man and that Stephens had recognized it at once.

"I started out with thirteen men," he said. "Our muskets were so old that they had to be fired with the lighted ends of cigars."

He pointed to some of the wounds he had received in battle, and added that he still had three musket balls embedded in his body.

His manner was easy and pleasant. Stephens got the impression that Carrera had changed his opinion of foreigners. Now out of the hills, Carrera had met and talked to people from other countries (an English doctor had even removed a musket ball from his side), and was much more friendly. Then, to Stephens' greater surprise, he said, "Foreigners are the only people who do not deceive me."

"You have a long career before you," Stephens told him. "You can do much good for your country."

Carrera laid his hand over his heart. "I am ready to give my life!"

"Your name has already reached my country. We have had in our newspapers an account of your last entry into Guatemala City. I believe our people praised you because you tried as much as you could to prevent cruel acts and killings."

Carrera smiled. "I am not a robber or a murderer. Those are things my enemies call me."

"You should travel in other countries, particularly in mine. It is so close."

"Ah, *si, Señor! El Norte!* When the wars are over, I will visit *El Norte.*"

Their conversation turned to war and to Morazán. Carrera warmed rapidly to both subjects; they were virtually all he knew. He spoke of things done and things yet to do. He told of his ambitions for Guatemala.

As Carrera talked, Stephens was almost persuaded that here was an honest man, a man of humble origin, a man denied the benefits of civilized society. Though he had never learned to write, Carrera could scribble his name. An aide looked quickly through some papers for an example of his signature but found none.

The more they talked of war, however, the more Carrera turned fanatical, even bloodthirsty. Stephens wondered if his violent outbursts could simply be a result of his own violent past. Somewhere in that past he had built up a hatred for white men; this hatred boiled over now and then but seemed mostly controlled. Stephens, quite unexpectedly, found himself admiring the boyish-looking leader.

"At parting," Stephens wrote, "he accompanied me to the door, and in the presence of his villainous soldiers made me a free offer of his services. I understood that I had had the good fortune to make a favorable impression; later, but unluckily during my absence, he called upon me in full dress and in state, which for him was an unusual thing."

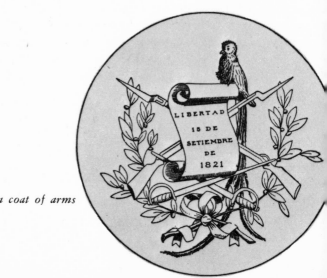

Guatemala coat of arms

6

EXPLORING CENTRAL AMERICA

JOHN Lloyd Stephens stayed in Guatemala City only long enough to gather information about the state of the government and to await Catherwood's arrival from Copán. It was hardly a dull wait. Swords rang in the street as adversaries clashed in the night. Injured men staggered through the alleys. Bursts of small-arms fire could be heard from near and far in the city.

To anyone else this might have seemed an excellent place to get out of. But not to Stephens. He ignored the public warnings against foreigners. Why flee? He was having a grand time!

Had anyone asked where he might be found during those days in Guatemala City, the response could well have been, "at the cockfight," "at the bullfight," "at the theater," or "gone to the Pacific."

His trip to the Pacific Ocean led him through the old, earthquake-shattered city of Antigua. Under a clear blue sky, the volcanoes of Agua and Fuego rose in green-clad beauty above the city. And, of course, the temptation was too much. He couldn't resist a day to climb the Volcán de Agua and explore its crater which he did, in the rain, slipping about ankle-deep in mud but satisfying his curiosity about the mountain.

Everywhere in Antigua itself, thanks to earthquakes and mudflows, he saw churches and convents crumbled into ruin. Homes were in shambles. Walls richly ornamented in stucco stood broken or cracked and leaning. Antiqua had not been completely deprived of people, however; it had

Cathedral at Antigua

been repopulated, and it presented to Stephens an aspect of both ruin and rejuvenation.

"The view was bounded on all sides by mountains of perpetual green," he wrote. "The morning air was soft and balmy, but pure and refreshing. With good government and laws, and one's friends around, I never saw a more beautiful spot on which man could desire to pass his allotted time on earth."

But his time in Antigua ended too soon. He had to leave this beautiful city and continue on his way to the sea. Astride a mule, and accompanied by a guide and servant, he rode out of Antigua, through a pass between the volcanoes, and to the edge of a broad tableland. From this high point he looked down to the west, to the jungles below. Far beyond, reflecting the tropic sun, lay the Pacific Ocean.

The trail down was shaded by trees—a blessing, as the air grew warmer with his descent—and hung with vines and creepers bearing red and purple flowers. Beautifully feath-

ered birds, including macaws in their brilliant garb of yellow, red, and green, flew among the trees. At his feet an
occasional scorpion scrambled out of the way. Iguanas three
feet long ran into the woods and disappeared.

The night was passed at Escuintla, deep in the coastal
jungle, and next morning—long before the sun was up—
Stephens and his party rode on toward the Pacific.

Very soon they heard waves breaking on the shore.
"The sound was grand and solemn," he wrote, "giving a
strong impression of the immensity of those waters which
had been rolling from the creation for more than five thousand years, unknown to civilized man. I was loth to disturb
the impression, and rode slowly through the woods, listen-
ing in profound silence to the grandest music that ever
fell upon my ear. . . . I had crossed the Continent of
America."

He returned to Guatemala City, along with others who
were going there to spend the Christmas holidays. Once

*Archway over street in Antigua. Volcano in background,
with summit hidden in clouds*

he passed a man and wife on horseback. The man carried a gamecock under his arm; the woman had a guitar. On the luggage mule a little boy was hidden, and in addition there were four boys walking, each with a gamecock under his arm. What festivities they would have!

Back in Guatemala City Stephens learned to his shock that Catherwood had been robbed by his servant. But the artist had not been harmed, and was, in fact, on his way to the city. On Christmas Day he arrived, "armed to the teeth," as Stephens described him, "pale and thin, and most happy at having reached Guatemala, but he was not half so happy as I was to see him."

Off they went with a party of Stephens' friends to the Plaza de Toros to watch a bullfight. There, once more, Stephens saw Carrera and his officers, who came in great pomp to watch the fight.

And then, almost before they realized it, a new year came.

"January 1, 1840. This day, so full of home associations—snow and red noses and blue lips out of doors, and blazing fires and beauteous faces within—opened in Guatemala like a morning in spring. The sun seemed to rejoice in the beauty of the land it shone upon. The flowers were blooming in the courtyards, and the mountains, visible above the tops of the houses, were smiling in verdure. The bells of thirty-eight churches and convents proclaimed the coming of another year."

Word came that Texas had invaded Mexico. Although Texas was not then a part of the United States of America, that country clearly approved of the invasion.

This made Guatemaltecos suspicious. If Mexico were invaded and conquered, what then? Might Guatemala be next?

This may have been why Stephens was looked upon in certain circles with mistrust. When the time came to travel south to El Salvador, Costa Rica, Nicaragua, and Honduras, in search of a government, he had difficulty obtaining a new endorsement for his passport. In some ways the situation was similar to that of modern times: a passport nowadays— in nearly all countries—is a small booklet in which certain countries require a rubber-stamp notation, or "visa," to be entered. Before the passport holder can travel in the foreign country, the visa must be stamped, approved, and signed by some official representing that country. Stephens was, no doubt, regarded by some Guatemalan officials as a "foreign-er," a spy. But at the last moment he managed to obtain the necessary endorsement, and Carrera even offered a troop escort, which Stephens declined.

On the fifth of January, Stephens and Catherwood departed from Guatemala City. Augustin had been discharged some weeks before, but they had a muleteer, and their need for a guide at the moment was not so pressing. They were traveling over ground that Stephens knew.

Under a scorching sun they headed south, off the plateau and down into the forested flatlands toward the Pacific Ocean. The shortest route would have been directly to El Salvador, but in the mountains were guerrillas who fought for no country, and who robbed and plundered and killed. Thus, using the better part of valor, Stephens decided to go by sea.

Once again he went alone, for Catherwood felt that his time could better be spent in Antigua—a city that any artist could love. With the ruins, the picturesque streets, and the volcanic landscape, he had enough to keep his pen and paintbrush busy. So, after seeing Stephens off at the port of Iztapa, he rode back up the mountain.

For Stephens, trouble began as soon as the ship had put to sea. A violent fever struck him, and an overpowering pain racked his head, rendering him helpless and sending him to bed. The attacks continued and were so severe that, when the ship arrived off the coast of El Salvador, he could not disembark. Besides, the weather was too hot for exertion of any kind.

Next day, he was carried ashore by the mate and some sailors. Walking feebly, he was led to a hut on a nearby *rancho* where hammocks had been hung. Into one of these he collapsed, with only an old woman of the *rancho* to care for him.

"It was close and hot," he wrote afterward, "but very soon I required all the covering I could get. I had a violent ague, followed by a fever, in comparison with which all I had suffered before was nothing. I called for water till the old woman was tired of giving it to me, and went out and left me alone. I became lightheaded, wild with pain, and wandered among the miserable huts with only the consciousness that my brain was scorching.

"I have an indistinct recollection of speaking English to some Indian women, of begging them to get me a horse to ride to Sonsonate; of some laughing, others looking at me with pity, and others leading me out of the sun and making me lie down under the shade of a tree. At three o'clock in the afternoon the mate came ashore again. I had changed my position, and he found me lying on my face asleep and almost withered by the sun.

"He wanted to take me back on board the ship, but I begged him to procure mules and take me to Sonsonate, within the reach of medical assistance. . . ."

After an agonizing mule ride of three hours—with the help of the mate—he arrived in Sonsonate. For three days he rested and at last began to regain his strength.

In this place, by good fortune, he met Don Diego Vigil, Vice-President of the United States of Central America.

Finally, here was a representative of the government he sought.

Don Diego was tall, thin, and about forty-five years old. Everything about him—his manner, his dress, his speech, the proud and dignified manner of the aristocrat—marked him as a gentleman.

"I am on my way to San Salvador, the capital," Stephens told him, keeping his language formal and diplomatic in tone. "I have credentials from the President of the United States of America. I fear, however, that in the current state of affairs I shall have difficulty in finding the government to which these credentials should be presented. Perhaps you can help me, *Señor*."

"*A sus ordenes, Señor*." ["At your service, sir."]

"Forgive me, sir, if I inquire whether the federal government exists. Perhaps the Republic is truly dissolved?"

"Señor Stephens," Don Diego replied, "I must tell you that the government exists, actually and legally. I myself am the duly elected Vice-President. Four of our states—including Guatemala—have declared themselves independent, which is unconstitutional. It is a rebellion. The Union cannot be dissolved except by a convention of deputies from all the states."

"And how much do you now control?"

"Three states. We shall soon have them all back. Is not your own state of South Carolina a little rebellious? And has not your Congress the right to force rebellious states to remain in the Union?"

"But do you have a Congress, Señor Vigil? Or a Cabinet? I am obliged to present my credentials to the Secretary of State—but have you one?"

"*Si, Señor*, here in Sonsonate, in my suite—an acting Secretary of State."

Don Diego informed Stephens that a convention was soon to be held in Honduras, where the difficulties of the Republic were to be resolved—or so he hoped.

As sincere as Don Diego seemed, his remarks left

Stephens uncertain, perplexed. The two parted on friendly
terms, but with the major question still unanswered: where
was the government? There was no point in presenting his
credentials to the Secretary of State if the very existence of
the State was in doubt.

From the window of his room in Sonsonate, Stephens
saw a magnificent sight—the volcano of Izalco. Explosive
eruptions could be heard at frequent intervals and, at night,
he saw molten lava burst out of the crater and roll down
the slope—a river of fire.

As usual, the sight of a volcano stretched his curiosity
to the breaking point. To Stephens, volcanoes were made
to be climbed!

Persuading an Irish merchant from Peru to accompany
him, he set out at dawn the next day. Past Indian villages
and through what he termed a forest of fruits and flowers,
they guided their horses up to a tableland from which they
had a view of the blue Pacific Ocean in the distance. Behind lay the jungle. Above rose Izalco, brown and barren,
more than 6,000 feet high. From here they saw that the
eruptions were too violent for anyone to climb the volcano

Izalco volcano, El Salvador

itself but, as usual, Stephens was not to be stopped. He saw a mountain above and behind Izalco. They would climb that instead.

With a loud report that sounded like a clap of thunder, the volcano exploded again. Black smoke and rock fragments, illuminated by flashes of orange flame, were hurled into the air. The earth shook. The horses snorted with uneasiness.

At eleven o'clock they sat by a stream and had lunch. It was the first time since leaving the ship—in fact since leaving Guatemala City—that Stephens had felt like eating anything.

After lunch they continued up the mountain, through a deep forest. "In a few minutes," Stephens wrote, "we came out suddenly upon an open point, higher than the top of the volcano, which commanded a view of the interior of the crater, and which was so near it that we saw the huge stones as they separated in the air and fell pattering around the sides of the volcano. In a few minutes our clothes were white with ashes, which fell around us with a noise like the sprinkling of rain."

Black and blue smoke blew out of the crater and rose in a towering column before them. Stones and ashes fell in showers. Then there was another flash, another explosion, another cloud flung aloft.

Stephens might have stayed all night to see this brilliant spectacle by dark. But they had no gear for sleeping on the mountain and so, with reluctance, turned and headed down across the lava flows to Sonsonate.

It was nearly midnight when they arrived. The evening ride through the forest was exhilarating, for behind them rose fiery pillars of smoke and ash, and bright streams of lava rolled down from the crater's edge. Thus did Izalco get its name—"Lighthouse of the Pacific."

For a man as weak with illness as Stephens, the day had

been a strenuous one. They had ridden more than fifty miles. But attacks of fever are no match for attacks of curiosity. As long as he could ride or walk or crawl, John Lloyd Stephens went in search of volcanoes or ancient ruins. Or governments.

It was in search of all three that he continued his journey. But now another important object of travel lured him south.

On January 22, 1840, Stephens and his guide left Sonsonate and shortly afterward embarked on another vessel

Route of Stephens' exploration of Central America in 1840

down the coast of Central America. Inland, beyond the shore, they could see the great volcanoes, one by one, a chain of them extending through El Salvador, Nicaragua, and Costa Rica.

As they approached the narrow waist of Central America, a slender isthmus of land which separated the Atlantic and Pacific oceans, Stephens had new dreams in mind—and not of Maya ruins.

"My principal object in leaving Sonsonate," he said, "had been to acquire some information in regard to the canal route between the Atlantic and Pacific by means of the Lake of Nicaragua and the River San Juan."

Perhaps it was only a dream. It had long been a dream of merchants and seafarers to construct a navigable canal across the narrow neck of land that linked the northern and southern American continents, a canal big enough for giant ocean-going vessels. Were such a canal to be built, the saving in time and money in traveling or in shipping goods between two ports, such as New York and San Francisco, would be tremendous.

At least it would be worth a try. The *route* of a canal could be scouted out, anyway, and then. . .

Always interested in seeing as much new country as possible, Stephens took the boat all the way to Puntarenas, in Costa Rica, planning to return by an inland route and explore the canal possibilities in Nicaragua on the way back to Guatemala.

Costa Rica at that time was one of the most prosperous states in the Union. Although it had had a revolution of its own, by and large the state had escaped the savage war that had so desecrated Guatemala.

As he rode through the green and flowering tropical forest, past coffee plantations, around ravines and beside volcanoes, Stephens sensed a different sort of excitement in the land.

Costa Rica did not seem to be going to ruin like the rest of Central America—here there were industry and activity rather than terror.

Practically every night Stephens had the problem of finding a place to stay. He never knew where he would sleep, or whether he would find any shelter at all. Few travelers came so far into the wild lands of Central America, and so there were no hotels, no tourist homes, hardly even a hut in which he could get some rest. Besides, the sight of him, perched atop his mule, bearded, clothing rumpled, and dust-covered from a day on the trail, his luggage piled on the mule behind him, might have frightened a prospective host.

But he managed. The lack of public accommodations never dampened his enthusiasm for the several tasks he pursued. Racked by fever again, he climbed the volcano of Cartago (now Irazú) from which he got a grand view of both the Pacific and the Atlantic oceans. He stopped at coffee plantations and stayed in convents and, not to neglect his diplomatic duty, made an official call on the head of the state.

Day by day, week after week, he wrote steadily in his notebook, keeping a detailed record of where he went and what he saw.

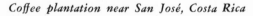

Coffee plantation near San José, Costa Rica

With the coming of February he bought two new mules and turned north on the route to Nicaragua. Altogether, in order to reach Guatemala and rejoin Catherwood, he would have to cover twelve hundred miles. It would be difficult riding in perilous country: rumors of war reached far into the jungle wilderness.

And wilderness it was—one of the wildest paths he had ever trod. Deer bounded through the forest. Turkeys flew overhead. Flocks of vultures sat in the trees. Stephens sometimes heard the barking of coyotes and the screaming of wildcats in the forest. At times the noise of locusts became loud and almost startling. Monkeys swinging through the trees sent locusts flying in swarms so great that Stephens and his guide had to beat the insects off with their hats. Once, in such a swarm, Stephens' mule snorted and violently pulled aside, ramming him against a tree.

"Well," he thought, "if this is the outset, what will be the end?"

At evening they searched for a *hacienda,* or a house or hut, where they could string their hammocks. They usually had dinner early—*tortillas,* rice, and a cup of chocolate—made and served by Nicolas, the guide. In the morning they arose before dawn and resumed their journey.

One evening at the hacienda of Santa Rosa they were welcomed by a gentleman named Don Juan José Bonilla, a member of one of the oldest families in Costa Rica. Because of political fortunes and misfortunes as well as changes in government, Don Juan had been forced into exile from time to time and was now in retirement in his home.

It was on this particular night that Stephens became abruptly familiar with another aspect of Central American life.

"While sitting at the supper table we heard a noise over our heads, which seemed to me like the opening of the roof. Don Juan threw his eyes to the ceiling and suddenly started from his chair, threw his arms around the neck of a servant, and with the fearful word *'temblor'!* [an earth-quake!] all rushed for the doors.

"I sprang from my chair, made one bound across the room, and cleared the piazza.

"The earth rolled like the pitching of a ship in a heavy sea. My step was high, my feet barely touched the ground and my arms were thrown up involuntarily to save myself from falling. I was the last to start, but, once under way, I was the last to stop.

"Halfway across the yard I stumbled over a man on his knees, and fell. I never felt myself so feeble a thing before. . . .

"The return of the earth to steadiness was almost as violent as the shock. We waited a few minutes after the last vibration, and then Don Juan said it was over and, assisted by his servant, he entered the house. I had been the last to leave it, but I was the last to return; and my chair lying with its back on the floor gave an intimation of the haste with which I had decamped."

If there wasn't one trouble, there was another. "Before the evening was over," said Stephens, "I forgot the earth-quake in a minor trouble. The uncultivated grounds of Central America teem with noxious insects. Riding all day in the woods, striking my head against the branches of trees had brought ticks down upon me in such numbers that I could brush them off with my hand.

"I had suffered so much during the day that twice I was obliged to strip at a stream and tear them out of my flesh, which gave me only temporary relief for lumps of irritation were left.

"In the midst of serious disquisitions with Don Juan, impolite as it was, I was obliged to use my nails violently and constantly. I was fain to entreat him to go out and give me the room to myself.

"A moment after he retired all my clothes were out of doors, and I tore the vipers out by the teeth; but Don Juan to my relief sent a deaf and dumb boy, who, by touching them with a ball of black wax, drew them from their burrowing places without any pain; yet they left behind wounds from which I did not recover in a long time."

Windstorms, dust clouds, grass fires, ticks, locusts, mosquitoes—despite all hardships, on went Stephens to the north, into the heart of Central America.

His spirits lifted when they came to Nicaragua. Here he would find out whether a canal between the Atlantic and Pacific was possible. He had read everything he could on the subject, both in England and the United States, and had talked with anyone who had had the slightest bit of information.

Now on the spot he felt a disappointment in the wildness and desolation of the land. The task of cutting through these hills and digging a wide canal—with shovels only—seemed almost insurmountable. Could it be done? Stopping briefly at the Pacific end of the proposed canal he was hard put to imagine that cities might one day rise in such a wilderness.

"But the scene was magnificent," he later recalled. "The sun was setting, and the high eastern headland threw a deep shade over the water. It was perhaps the last time in my life that I should see the Pacific; and in spite of fever and ague tendencies, I bathed once more in the great ocean."

He examined, as best he could, the route a canal might follow from the Pacific to Lake Nicaragua. But inquiries to local people about digging a canal did little good; no one in Nicaragua seemed to know anything about the canal or the rock through which it would have to be dug. No one, that is, except Baily.

John Baily was a British naval officer who had been

hired two years before by the Central American government to make a survey of the canal route. He had almost
completed his survey when the civil war broke out.

Stephens met Baily in Granada, a city on the shore of
Lake Nicaragua, and for hours the two of them talked about
the canal route. From the Pacific Ocean, Baily said, the
canal would have to be cut through fifteen miles of flat
land and low hills to Lake Nicaragua. Beyond the eastern
edge of this lake a river, flowing some seventy-nine miles to
the Atlantic, could be utilized.

The biggest question was how much the digging would
cost. Baily had found what Stephens suspected: the price
of a canal would be high, perhaps too high. The estimated
cost of construction was twenty to twenty-five million
dollars.

Stephens copied in his journal all the facts and figures he
could. Whatever the expense of the enterprise, it was still
worth looking into. Others had been looking into it. Columbus had sought a way through the land that separated him
from the East Indies. The Spanish had conducted a survey
during their domination of Central America, but little had
come of it. Someone had also investigated the narrower,
more southerly Isthmus of Panama, but concluded that a
canal there would be quite impossible to build.

Then the United States of Central America had revived
the plans to build a canal, and had hired Baily. But now
the war—not canals—was on the minds of the people.

7

REBELLION

RIDING north in Nicaragua, Stephens climbed the volcanoes of Masaya and Coseguina. The farther north they went, the more war rumors they heard. General Morazán was supposed to be not far distant with his army. That meant more fighting, and in the towns and villages people were uneasy.

Stephens and his guide and muleteer heard the tramp of cavalry in the streets and saw barefooted soldiers marching north. If only the road to Guatemala would stay open.

For miles the road lay over dark volcanic soil. North out of Nicaragua, through a short section of Honduras and into El Salvador, they guided their horses, passing the volcanoes of San Miguel, San Vicente, and San Salvador.

Day after day they rode along the dusty or muddy roads, into valleys, past immense ravines, and through deep forests. In villages they came upon typical scenes of women filling their water jars or washing clothes, men bathing, and horses and mules drinking at a common fountain. The life of these people seemed easy-going; their wants appeared to be few and easily supplied. Yet in the unsettled state of the country, they knew that war could come their way at any time. For some it had already arrived.

Soldiers of Honduras were on the march. Advancing into El Salvador, which was in a state of arms against the Union, the rebels rode furiously, with slashing machetes, striking terror into the villagers. People fled as fast as they could to villages beyond the line of march, or into the mountains to hide until the fighting ceased.

A village well

Stephens came to huts and sheds that were filled with frightened fugitives. He saw trembling families gathered under trees, waiting for the worst.

At last he entered the city of San Salvador, capital of the Republic—or capital of whatever republic remained. San Salvador had recently been shaken and nearly destroyed by an earthquake. Along the hot and dusty streets Stephens guided his horse among heaps of rubbish and in front of houses with their facades cracked and falling. Then, in the central part of town and along the approaches to the plaza he came to barricades and cannons and soldiers.

Seeing that the war was rapidly growing more intense, Stephens called on Vice-President Vigil, from whom he learned that Carrera had conquered the province of Quezaltenango and annexed it to Guatemala.

At that very moment, General Morazán was on his way

to Guatemala—and rebels were on the way to San Salvador.
"In the midst of this confusion," Stephens wrote, "where
was my government? I had traveled all over the country,
led on by a glimmering light shining and disappearing, and
I could not conceal from myself that the crisis of my fortune was at hand.

"All depended upon the success of Morazán's expedition.
If he failed, my occupation was gone; but in this darkest
hour of the Republic I did not despair. In ten years of war
Morazán had never been beaten. Carrera would not dare
fight him. Guatemala would fall. The moral effect would
be felt all over the country: Quezaltenango would shake
off its chains; the strong minority in the other states would
rise; the flag of the Republic would once more wave tri-
umphantly; and out of chaos the government I was in search
of would appear."

But would it? He had no intention of waiting until the
government came to him. If he waited too long, the road
to Guatemala would be cut off, and that would cut off the
road to more of the ancient ruins. Hunting a phantom government had its exciting moments, but such a chase was
also vexing. It could last for years. And anyone who was at
all acquainted with Stephens knew that he would rather
be hunting Maya ruins.

Suddenly there was a clatter in the streets. Twenty
horsemen galloped into the city with news that Honduras
troops were marching directly upon the capital and would
arrive within a few hours.

What luck! thought Stephens. For days he had been
just ahead of these troops. Now that they were about to
arrive he would stay and watch the action.

He had no excuse for remaining, except his own interest.
His passport was complete. The mules were loaded and
ready. A sea captain, whose leaky boat was up for sale, had
joined Stephens for the final ride to Guatemala City. He

was anxious to depart; he had on his spurs and sword and was waiting, when Stephens told him the news of the approaching troops.

"*Carramba!*" said the captain, mounting his mule as fast as he could. "Thank God we are ready. *Vámonos!*"

"*Un minuto*," said Stephens. "Not so fast. I intend to remain."

The captain wheeled his mule and looked down at the New Yorker as if in disbelief. "Remain here?"

"Yes, why not?"

"You are made, my *norteamericano* friend! You do not know these soldiers as I do. They are bandits, killers—"

"Yes, I know. I still intend to stay."

The captain flung back his head. "Well, not I! Up the road a few leagues is a *hacienda*. I wait for you there."

"Very well," said Stephens. "Take the pack mules and the servants. I shall join you as soon as I can."

As the captain spurred his mule out of town, Stephens turned and rode through the streets of San Salvador amid preparations for war.

Men loaded pistols and fastened their spurs. Drums beat in the streets, calling volunteers to defend the city. Soldiers mounted their horses and galloped off to take up positions at the edge of town. The city became still and quiet.

When news arrived that the invading soldiers had stopped just short of the city, two hundred mounted soldiers gave a war whoop and rode out of town to attack.

Disappointed, Stephens turned back to his mule. Unable to wait any longer, he mounted and "left my capital to its fate, even yet uncertain whether I had any government."

As he rode out of San Salvador and caught up with the captain and the servants, he knew perfectly well that he was not leaving all the danger behind. If Morazán's soldiers had cleared the road to Guatemala City, Stephens would have some prospect of getting through without attack by bandits. But that was no certainty. He knew that, as they rode north, they could be ambushed anywhere, any time. Terrorists still hid in the hills and the villages. As in any state of anarchy, the absence of government encouraged lawlessness. Stephens never knew around what bend of the trail they might be robbed or shot.

The little party arrived in Sonsonate, where tumult reigned because of a rumor that Carrera had left Guatemala with an army of two thousand men to march upon El Salvador. If so, they might have already met Morazán. Perhaps a battle was even then under way.

Next morning, in darkness, the little party climbed into saddles and rode out of Sonsonate. A bright red river of fire streamed down the slope of Izalco—hot and violent as the passions of war that rolled over Central America.

Central plaza of San Salvador, El Salvador, in 1960

As day came, new trouble threatened. They had been unable to secure pack mules in the regions through which they passed, and they had had no recourse but to overload the mules they had.

"Our mules presented a piteous spectacle," Stephens said. "Mine, which had carried my light luggage like a feather . . . had gone on with admirable steadiness up hill and down dale, but when we stopped she trembled in every limb, and before the cargo was removed I expected to see her fall.

"Nicolas and the muleteer said she would certainly die, and the faithful brute seemed to look at me reproachfully for having suffered so heavy a load to be put upon her back. I tried to buy or hire another, but all were removed one or two days' journey out of the line of march of the soldiers."

It was dark as they entered the village of Ahuachapán, where the people waited tensely for word from Guatemala. Very shortly it came.

Two soldiers rode into town with the news that Morazán had been defeated in his attack on Guatemala. His army had been cut to pieces.

Now Stephens' fears were realized. The soldiers, routed and disbanded, would sweep every road and every trail, robbing merchants, murdering travelers, terrorizing villages.

"*La gente viene!*" A soldier galloped down the darkened street, sword flying, spurs rattling, shouting at the top of his voice. "They're coming!"

Chaos reigned over the village. Church bells tolled wildly. A horseman with a flying red banner on his lance clattered through the town warning everyone to flee. By moonlight, men raced from their houses and leaped upon horses. Women with large bundles moved as fast as they could, pushing their children before them.

By sunrise the village was virtually deserted. No dogs barked. No roosters crowed. Not a sound could be heard.

The dust of the day before had settled, and even the air was still. To Stephens it was as if he suddenly owned a village and the people had fled in terror from his property.

A little boy ran up to him and said that the soldiers could be seen approaching. Stephens climbed the church steeple to see for himself, and sure enough, there was a forward company of Carrera's army descending a hill in single file, muskets flashing in the sun.

By the time they entered the village, Stephens and the captain were out in the street to meet them.

"Where is the commander of this village?" asked a scout.

"Seek him in the mountains," the captain replied.

Stephens spoke up. "Who is your general?"

"General Figueroa," answered the soldier. "We wait for battle."

Stephens smiled. "Well, you will not find it here. The village has only old men and women and children in it, and few of them. We are travelers. If you wish someone to surrender the village to you—why, we shall do it!"

The general, braced with pistols and a sword but no uniform, marched his company into the village—and a ragged company it was! Lancers on horseback, looking carefully around as if expecting an ambush; half-naked, barefoot Indians wearing old straw hats and brandishing machetes and muskets.

"*Viva Carrera!*" they shouted.

"*Viva Carrera!*" responded Stephens. He was hardly a devoted follower of the Guatemala ruler, but he did not mind shouting "*Viva Carrera!*" He would have been shot on the spot if he hadn't.

After the soldiers had stacked their muskets in the plaza, Stephens sought out the general. "He was a young man— all the men in that country were young—about thirty-two or three, dressed in a snuff-colored cloth roundabout jacket with pantaloons of the same color; off his warhorse and away from his assassin-like band, he had very much the air of an honest man."

"*Señor Ministro de Norte América.*" That was how the general introduced Stephens to the other officers. And then Stephens, playing his role of diplomat to the full, invited the general and all his officers to breakfast. It was a bold stroke on his part. There was no food in the village, and the officers had not eaten since the day before. They accepted at once.

And so vanished Stephens' small stock of provisions for the road. But thanks to this courtesy, he got his passport signed by the general—an extra precaution.

It was almost dark by the time Stephens, the captain, Nicolas, and the muleteer were ready to leave. All of a sudden they saw soldiers grabbing muskets and leaping on their horses. General Figueroa galloped down the street and pulled up in front of them.

"General Morazán is coming!" he shouted. "He is almost here. We are going out to meet him. When you get to Guatemala City, call upon President Carrera and pay my respects." He held out his hand. "*Hasta luego!*"

They shook hands, after which the general wheeled his horse and dashed along the line of lancers. Once more Stephens and the captain watched the ragged soldiers pass —only this time they were returning from whence they came.

"*Viva Carrera!*" they shouted.

"*Viva Carrera!*" Stephens and the captain replied.

"The last of the line had hardly disappeared," Stephens later wrote in describing the events of the day, "before we heard a volley of musketry, and in a moment the fifty or sixty men left in the plaza snatched up their arms and ran down a street opening from the plaza.

"Very soon a horse without a rider came clattering down the street at full speed; three others followed, and in five minutes we saw thirty or forty horsemen with our friend Figueroa at their head dash across the street, all running for their lives; but in a few moments they rallied and returned.

"We were walking toward the church to ascend the steeple when a sharp volley of musketry rolled up the street on that side; and before we got back into the house there was firing along the whole length of the street. Knowing that a chance shot might kill a non-combatant, we secured the doors and windows. Finally, however, as the firing was sharp and the balls went beyond us and struck the houses on the opposite side . . . we retired into a small room on the courtyard, with delightful walls and a bullet-proof door three inches thick.

"Shutting the door, we listened valiantly in utter darkness. Here we considered ourselves out of harm's way, but we had serious apprehensions for the result. The spirit on both sides was to kill; giving quarter was not thought of. Morazán's party was probably small, but they would not be taken without a desperate fight, and from the sharpness of the firing and the time occupied, there was probably a sanguinary affair going on. . . .

"I never felt more relieved than when we heard the sound of a bugle. It was the Morazán blast of victory. . . .

"Very soon we heard the tramp of cavalry, and leaving our hiding place, we returned to the *sala* and heard a cry of *Viva la Federación!* This was a cheering sound.

"It was now dark. We opened the door an inch or two, but a lancer riding by struck it wide open with his lance and asked for water. We gave him a large calabash, which another took from his hands. We threw open the door and kept two large calabashes on the sill, and the soldiers, as they passed, took a hasty draught. Asking a question of each, we learned that it was General Morazán himself with the survivors of his own expedition against Guatemala. . . .

"The soldiers marched into the plaza, stacked their arms, and shouted *Viva Morazán!* In the morning the shout had been *Viva Carrera!*"

In a few moments a party of officers, some of them wounded, arrived and entered the courtyard of the house. They struck Stephens as being the finest set of men he had seen in the country.

But how bitter they were! In describing their battles, said Stephens, "they talked only of killing; taking prisoners was never thought of. The verb *matar* (to kill) with its inflections was so continually ringing in my ears that it made me nervous."

Morazán was to stay in the plaza. Here at last was a chance to meet the famous general. As Stephens made his way to the plaza, he saw at once the difference between Morazán's men and those of Carrera. Morazán's soldiers had discipline. They did not sack the town or disturb the people. On the contrary, they were hungry and tired, and most of them were stretched out on the ground, sound asleep.

Morazán himself stood in one of the buildings, near a table with a candle on it. He was slender, of medium height, and wore a mustache. His face supported a full growth of beard. He must have been about 45 years old, according to Stephens' guess. He wore a military coat buttoned to the throat, and carried a sword.

There was a mild, intelligent bearing about him, which seemed to belie the almost legendary tales of bravery and fierce battles he had fought. Morazán, with great military skill, always led his troops in person and had been wounded frequently. To the people of Central America—or at least to those who begged him to save them—he was a hero.

As they shook hands, the general asked: "My family— do you know whether they arrived in Costa Rica?"

Stephens replied that he did not know.

The general's face was impassive. "I am sorry, señor,

Francisco Morazán

for the condition of my country. Your visit is at a most un-
fortunate moment. I wish that a new treaty between your
country and mine could have been prepared. But now I
fear it is too late. . . ."

He paused and closed his eyes. He was exhausted. After
a few words more, Stephens withdrew.

Next morning, Morazán called upon Stephens. They talked at first about Carrera, but then the general said, "Señor Stephens, I would consider it unsafe for you to go to Guatemala City."

"The captain and I are anxious to set out," said Stephens. "My work has nearly ended in your country and I am anxious to explore ancient ruins in Guatemala and Mexico."

"I would give you an escort of soldiers," replied Morazán, "but that in itself would expose you to danger. You seem to know how to get along on your own in our unhappy land. I will ask the *alcalde* to provide you a guide."

They shook hands and said good-by. Morazán left.

How strange are the twists of fate in this world. Stephens could not have known what troubles Morazán was still to face in trying to reunite his country, or that his soldiers and his people would eventually desert him, and that, at the end, with his country in ruins, he would sail away to join his family in Chile, four thousand miles to the south.

"He is now fallen and in exile," Stephens was to write, later that year, "probably forever, and under sentence of death if he returns. . . . But I verily believe they have driven from their shores the best man in Central America."

In defiance of Morazán's warning, Stephens began the long and dangerous trip to Guatemala City. Shortly after entering Guatemala, and thus reentering territory occupied by Carrera's troops, the party approached a *hacienda* one evening. On the porch sat three soldiers eating *tortillas*.

"They saw us at the same moment," wrote Stephens, "snatched up their muskets, and ran; but suddenly one stopped and leveled at us a blunderbuss. The barrel looked as big as a church door, and seemed to cover both the captain and me. We were in awful danger of being shot by mistake when one of them rushed back, knocked up the blunderbuss, and cried out, 'Amigos, los ingleses! [the Englishmen!].'"

8

ESCAPE INTO MEXICO

"AND now I would fain let the reader sit down and enjoy himself quietly in Guatemala, but I cannot. The place did not admit of it. I could not conceal from myself that the federal government was broken up; there was not the least prospect of its ever being restored, nor, for a long time to come, of any other being organized in its stead.

"Under these circumstances I did not consider myself justified in remaining any longer in the country. I was perfectly useless for all the purposes of my mission, and I made a formal return to the authorities of Washington, in effect, 'after diligent search, no government found.'

"I was once more my own master, at liberty to go where I pleased, at my own expense, and immediately we commenced making arrangements for our journey to Palenque."

There was no time to lose. Palenque, a name given to a Mexican village and the Indian ruins near it, lay far to the north over roads that became impassable during the rainy season. And the rainy season was approaching.

Worse yet, Indians in the highlands along the way were now said to be in a state of uprising and, in fact, had already murdered some travelers. Who could say when the road would be completely blocked and every stranger ambushed?

Nevertheless, the fame of the ruins—mysterious as they were—had spread throughout the world. The Mexican village of Palenque had been founded in the sixteenth century. But many years had passed, perhaps 200, before anyone knew that a great Maya city lay buried in the jungle just a few leagues away. The ruins near Palenque had been "discovered" some time during the eighteenth century, and reports of magnificent architecture had reached the outside world on several occasions. How could anyone visit Mexico without seeing Palenque?

The only trouble was that Palenque was so remote, so far back in the mountains, that few travelers ever got there. Deep canyons, muddy trails, sheer cliffs. . . .

The friends Stephens had made in Guatemala City begged him not to go. So convincing were they, he said, that "we almost shrunk from our purpose. I have no hesitation in saying that it was a matter of most serious consideration whether we should not abandon it altogether and go home; but we had set out to go to Palenque, and we could not return without seeing it."

At this point, Catherwood arrived from Antigua, and the two literally fell into each other's arms, as if they were long-lost brothers. They resolved that from that moment on, in this war-torn land, they would stick together and not separate again.

Stephens spent hours telling Catherwood how he had gone by sea to Costa Rica, climbed volcanoes, suffered attacks of malaria, traveled through magnificent jungles, got caught in battles, and finally met Morazán. Catherwood himself had new drawings to show Stephens. He had even returned to Copán on a visit, and had explored Quiriguá, a site of Maya ruins near the Motagua River.

With his partner safe and the southern trip over, Stephens could relax a little. Once again, with sheer delight, he gazed out over the houses, streets, and churches of Guatemala City.

"It looked beautiful," he wrote. "I never thought I should be so happy to see it again. I had finished a journey of twelve hundred miles, and the gold of Peru could not have tempted me to undertake it again."

But, alas, he saw marks of war that had not been there when he left. With a touch of sorrow he walked along the streets for the last time, and stood on the plaza breathing the pure mountain air. He could not help feeling sad that so beautiful a city—and country—lay in such distress.

He paid a final call on Carrera and, as before, was received in a friendly manner. This time he obtained a passport personally signed by the chief which, he hoped, would pass him safely among the warlike Indians who revered Carrera.

Diplomacy over, Stephens and Catherwood packed their mules with utmost care for the difficult, hazardous, extended journey ahead. Each had two leather trunks, which were lashed to the sides of the pack mules. Into the trunks went hammocks, blankets, sheets, pillows, food, and medi-

Mozo on road

cal supplies. Other things that had been collected on their travels to this point, but which would not be needed from here on, were shipped directly home.

Stephens and Catherwood had six animals altogether— a mule for each to ride, a pack mule for each, a spare pack mule, and a horse for relief. In addition, their party consisted of two *mozos,* or servant lads, who would do a great deal of the cooking, packing, loading, and odd jobs required on such an expedition.

On April 17, 1840, they said *adiós* to their friends and set out from Guatemala City on the mountain road to Mexico. They rose along the slopes of tumbling hills and rode through deep, rich forests at the edges of ravines and canyons. (See map in Chapter 12.)

Stephens does not say that they stopped and looked back down upon the city spread out in the valley below them, but very likely they did, for it is a magnificent view. They had been too long here and had had too many adventures not to have stopped once more, not to have felt a certain sadness in leaving.

But now they were on the trail again, and that helped temper their sadness!

Climbing higher along winding paths, they saw fields of

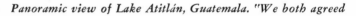

Panoramic view of Lake Atitlán, Guatemala. "We both agreed

corn, huts hidden in the trees, and collections of houses that made up villages large and small. And wherever there was the slightest evidence of prehistoric Indian ruins—or even a rumor about them—Stephens and Catherwood stopped to investigate.

After several days of travel they arrived at the edge of a great volcanic crater.

"At two o'clock we came out upon the lofty table of land bordering the Lake of Atitlán," Stephens wrote. "In general I have forborne attempting to give any idea of the magnificent scenery amid which we were traveling, but here forbearance would be a sin. . . .

"We looked down upon a surface shining like a sheet of molten silver; it was enclosed by rocks and mountains of every form, some barren and some covered with verdure. . . . Opposite, down on the borders of the lake, and apparently inaccessible by land, was the town of Santiago

that it was the most magnificent spectacle we ever saw."

Atitlán. . . . It was situated between two immense volcanoes . . . and farther on was another volcano, and farther still, another more lofty than all, with its summit
buried in clouds.

"There were no associations connected with this lake;
until lately we did not know it even by name; but we both
agreed that it was the most magnificent spectacle we ever
saw.

"We stopped and watched the fleecy clouds of vapor
rising from the bottom, moving up the mountains and the
sides of the volcanoes. . . . All the requisites of the grand
and beautiful were there: gigantic mountains, a valley of
poetic softness, lake and volcanoes; and from the eminence
on which we stood a waterfall marked a silver line down
its side."

Villages of the Indians clung to the slopes of the crater
or lay along the edge of the lake, dreamlike, as if built in
tropical gardens.

Jolting down the dusty trail to the bottom, Stephens and
Catherwood reveled in a refreshing swim. On the following
day they tried to cross the lake in a canoe, to visit the village of Santiago Atitlán, but the wind arose and they were
driven back to shore.

Stephens could have spent weeks at Lake Atitlán. The
geology of this volcanic land, the history, the Indians—
everything fascinated him. Unhappily, however, with all
the dangers ahead, he knew they must not delay.

Aboard their mules again, they climbed the narrow trail,
skirting waterfalls and edging along steep cliffs, up out of
the crater. On top, they halted for one last look at Lake
Atitlán. "From the moment this lake first opened upon us
until we left it," Stephens wrote, "our ride along it presented a greater combination of beauties than any locality
I ever saw."

The farther north they went, the more mountainous the

country became, and the more fierce the climate. At the edge of awesome canyons and steep-walled ravines that were hundreds of feet deep they were assailed by powerful blasts of wind. Very often the trails, for the most part rough and wild and tangled, led through a forest of rich vegetation, requiring hours of tortuous climbing up steep and hazardous slopes.

More than anything else, they sought out ruins—asking whatever Indians they met, and inquiring of the *padres* in every village. Ruins there were in plenty—ancient palaces and temples, mounds, platforms, terraces—but most of these were badly fallen apart. Worse yet, a great many stones from them had been taken away to be used in the construction of present-day buildings.

Even so, nothing they saw compared, so they were told, with the mysterious Palenque.

Names of the Guatemala cities they passed had magical, musical sounds, such as Quezaltenango, Huehuetenango, and Santo Tomás Chichicastenango. The latter town, now called simply Chichicastenango, is one of the most colorful and popular—to visitors—in Guatemala today. It is particularly famous for its central square. On market day, twice a week, Maya Indians come from miles around to sell their wares, to talk, to pray at the cathedral, and to listen to the music of several marimba orchestras. It was in Chichicastenango that Stephens saw a man and a boy whipped at a public whipping post—punishment that shocked him because of its barbaric nature.

The Indians, of course, spoke little or no Spanish, but rather dialects of Maya language. They had no grammar books, and not even a dictionary, but priests had transformed some of the sounds into alphabetical form. This so captured Stephens' attention that he copied a Maya version of the Lord's Prayer, which started out thus:

"*Cacahan chicah lae coni Vtzah. Vcahaxtizaxie mayih*

Bila Chipa ta pa Cani Ahauremla Chibantah. Ahuamla Uaxale Chiyala Chiqueeh hauta Vleus quehexi Caban Chicah. . . ."

The language, the cities, the scenery—Stephens sighed in both pleasure and dismay. So much to see and so little time! If only he could spend a month at each place! But they were pressing so steadily forward now that they did not have time to rest.

"There was a wild novelty, something that touched the imagination, in every step of our journey in that country. The old padre, in the deep stillness of the dimly lighted convent, with his long black coat like a robe, and his flashing eye, called up an image of the bold and resolute priests who accompanied the armies of the conquerors; as he drew

Village square at Chichicastenango

a map on the table and pointed out the sierra to the top of which he had climbed, and the position of the mysterious city, the interest awakened in us was the most thrilling I ever experienced."

To no one's surprise, the mules often slipped, stumbled, and staggered under their heavy loads. One became badly crippled in a fall. At other times, the mules were set upon by flies so fiercely that their heads and necks and sides were running with blood, which almost drove the animals frantic.

"The road was indeed rough and wild beyond all description," Stephens wrote, "and very soon, after reaching and descending another immense ravine, we commenced an ascent on the opposite side, which occupied three hours. Through openings in the woods we looked down precipices one or two thousand feet deep, with the mountainside still higher above us. The whole mountain was clothed with luxuriant vegetation, and though wanting the rocky, savage grandeur of Alpine scenery, at every turn the view was sublime."

On approaching the Mexican border, the little party was joined by a young American who gave his name as Henry Pawling. Stephens had seen him before, near Guatemala City, where Pawling had been the manager of a plantation. The newcomer wore a lengthy beard that seemed to age him considerably, though he was still in his twenties. Originally a New Yorker like Stephens, he had been traveling in Mexico and Guatemala for seven years. In that time he had nearly forgotten how to speak English.

"He had heard of our setting out for Mexico," Stephens wrote, "and, disgusted with his occupation and the country, had mounted his horse, and with all he was worth tied on behind his saddle, pushed on to overtake us. On the way he had bought a fine mule, and by hard riding, and changing from one animal to the other, he had reached us in four days. He was in difficulty about a passport, and was anxious

to have the benefit of mine in order to get out of the country, offering to attach himself to me in any capacity necessary for that purpose. Fortunately, my passport was broad
enough to cover him, and I immediately constituted him
the general manager of the expedition."

The wilderness country through which they traveled
was rugged and gentle by turns. The little party descended
over tortuous trails into yawning canyons whose depths
were lost in shadow and whose walls rose sheer and towering above.

"Before us," Stephens wrote, "between these immense
walls was a vista reaching beyond the village of San Andrés, twenty-four miles distant. A stream of water was dash-
ing down over rocks and stones, hurrying on to the Atlantic;
we crossed it perhaps fifty times on bridges wild and rude
as the stream itself and the mountains between which it
rolled. As we descended, the temperature became milder.

"At twelve o'clock the immense ravine opened into a
rich valley a mile in width, and in half an hour we reached
the village of Todos Santos. On the right, far below us, was
a magnificent table cultivated with corn and bounded by
the side of the great sierra; and in the suburbs of the village
were apple and peach trees covered with blossoms and
young fruit.

"We had again reached the *tierras templadas* [cultivated
fields], and in Europe or North America the beauty of this
miserable unknown village would be a theme for poetry."

A short distance beyond the village of Santiago Petatán
they were almost trapped by a forest fire.

"We turned back and attempted to pass by another road,
but were unable. Before we returned, the fire had reached
the place we left, and it increased so fast that we had apprehensions for the luggage mules, and we hurried them
back with the men toward the village.

"The flames came creeping and crackling toward us, shooting up and whirled by currents of wind, and occasionally, when fed with dry and combustible materials, flashing, and darting along like a train of gunpowder.

"We fell back, keeping as near as we could to the line of fire. The road lay along the side of a mountain; the fire came from the ravine below, crossing the road and moving upward. The clouds of smoke and ashes, the rushing of currents of wind and flames, the crackling of burning branches and trees wrapped in flames, and the rapid progress of the destroying element, made such a wild and fearful scene that we could not tear ourselves away.

"At length we saw the flames rush up the side of the ravine, intercepting the path before us. We spurred our horses, shot by, and in a moment the whole was a sheet of flame.

"The fire was now spreading so rapidly that we became alarmed. We hurried back to the church, which, on an elevation strongly defined against the immense mountain in the background, stood before us as a place of refuge.

"By this time the villagers had become alarmed, and men and women were hurrying to the height to watch the progress of the flames. The village was in danger of conflagration; it would be impossible to urge the loaded mules up the hill we had descended, so we resolved to deposit the luggage in the church and save the mules by driving them up unburdened.

"It was another of those wild scenes to which no effect can be given in words. We stopped on the brow of the hill before the square of the church and, while we were watching the fire, the black clouds and sheets of flame rolled up the side of the mountain and spared the village. Relieved from apprehension, we sat down under a tree in front of the church to the calm enjoyment of the terrific spectacle and a cold fowl. The cinders and ashes fell around, and the destructive element rushed on, sparing the village before us, perhaps to lay some other to ruins."

Crossing primitive bridges, riding narrow trails, swimming mountain streams, they made their way into Mexico and closer to Palenque—closer also to a new batch of troubles.

It was the old question of a passport. They had to get one soon or they dared not travel farther into Mexico. Finding a military outpost, they succeeded in getting one that would do, thanks to Stephens' official position.

And more trouble: while most of Mexico was at peace, some parts of the country into which they rode remained in a state of revolution. It was as they had feared. They had been warned about this in Guatemala City. But you can almost see the smile on Stephens' face, and can almost guess his thoughts: we went through a Central American revolution and came out alive; we will not be stopped by a Mexican one!

Nevertheless, they had to keep watch. And furthermore, they were proceeding with full knowledge of a Mexican order forbidding strangers to visit the ruins of Palenque. Stephens had dismissed that matter quickly:

"If we apply to the government for permission to go there," he said, "we'll be refused. Therefore, we'll not apply."

"And if we are caught?" someone asked.

"Turning back is not in our vocabulary." Stephens had said it before; he meant it here just as strongly. "We cannot take time to go all the way to Mexico City to get a permit."

"Then—" said Pawling, "what are our chances?"

"We know," said Stephens, "that the ruins are remote, not near habitation, except for the village of Palenque. I doubt that the government has any spare soldiers to station there as guards, what with the revolution going on. I venture to say that the ruins will be deserted. Once we get there, we can explore all we wish and then be gone before anyone knows we are in the neighborhood. If someone happens to discover us, we have only to plead ignorance. The worst they can do—I trust—is ask us to leave."

He turned his mule down the trail, saying over his shoulder, "It will be worth the risk if we get just one day's quiet possession, *amigos: Vámonos!*"

They passed through "soft and lovely valleys," as Stephens called them, where chapel bells tolled and called the Indian people to evening prayer. Then they headed off into mountains more rugged than any they had seen.

Unluckily, just as they did so, the rainy season broke. Thunder crashed among the barren crags and filled the canyons with booming echoes. Rain swept by in sheets, the earth became muddy, and the road turned into a soggy, slippery quagmire. With still worse roads ahead, Stephens and Catherwood must have looked at each other as if to say, "Mico Mountain all over again?"

Day after day, rain after rain, they slogged onward—or more correctly, upward and downward. Despite the downpours, they continued to investigate whatever ruins lay along the route and, near Ococingo, stopped to examine the ruins of Toniná. Riding up the terraces of a stone-faced, stuccoed pyramid, they stopped, tied their horses, and climbed among lemon trees to the temple on top. It was a large building composed of several chambers that had collapsed into rubble.

Rumor had it that one of the openings here, beneath a doorway, opened into a cave that led all the way to Palenque. Their guide swore that the story was true. If Stephens thought it absurd, he made no mention.

"A short cut to Palenque is exactly what we wanted," he

Turkey buzzard

wrote, "so I took off my coat and, lying down on my breast, began to crawl under. When I had advanced about half the length of my body, I heard a hideous hissing noise and, starting back, saw a pair of small eyes, which in the darkness shone like balls of fire.

"The precise portion of time that I employed in backing out is not worth mentioning. My companions had heard the noise, and the guide said it was *un tigre.* I thought it was a wildcat; but, whatever it was, we determined to have a shot at it.

"We took it for granted that the animal would dash past us, and in a few moments our guns and pistols, swords and machetes were ready. When we had taken our positions . . . out fluttered a huge turkey buzzard, which flapped itself through the building and took refuge in another chamber."

As they continued on their way toward Palenque, villagers warned them that once they got across the mountains the rainy season would trap them. The message was perfectly clear. There was no coming back from Palenque.

This stopped Pawling in his tracks. He would go anywhere else in Mexico—but he had not bargained for this!

Stephens reminded him of the revolution and the renegade Indians in these hills, saying that Pawling needed the company and protection of the whole party just as the party needed his pistols and double-barreled shotgun. As if to underscore the point, they met with menacing stares in some of the mountain villages they passed.

"The country through which we were now traveling," Stephens wrote in his notebook, "was as wild as before the Spanish conquest, and without a habitation until we reached Palenque. The road was through forest so overgrown with brush and underwood as to be impenetrable; the branches were trimmed barely high enough to admit a man's traveling under them on foot, so that on the backs of our mules we were constantly obliged to bend our bodies and even to dismount."

To prying eyes, theirs must have seemed an odd procession. Four Indians, each with a chained and padlocked oxhide box on his back, led the way; then came one of the servants, clad only in a hat and cotton breeches, driving two mules and carrying a double-barreled gun; next in line were Stephens, Catherwood, and Pawling, each leading his mule; and finally other Indian bearers and some Indian boys.

So steep did the trail become that Stephens and his colleagues agreed to mount a chair on the backs of the bearers and allow themselves to be carried along the trail. After all, it was the custom in this part of the world to do so.

As Stephens climbed aboard the Indian, the fellow staggered under the weight. Then he approached the edge of a canyon more than a thousand feet in depth.

"Here I became anxious to dismount," said Stephens, in one of the greatest understatements of his career.

The Indian cautiously placed each foot in position as he walked, testing every stone to see if it were solid, and to see if it would support their weight. He stepped to the edge of the precipice, trembling. Stephens was sure that the fellow's knees would fail and they would both go tumbling into the chasm.

Now the Indian picked his way along the very edge. Stephens froze in position, one leg dangling over empty space. He dared not move a muscle lest he disturb the bearer's delicate balance and thus precipitate them over the cliff. He would have given the gold of Mexico to be off that bearer's back!

"To my extreme relief," he wrote, "the path finally turned away; but I had hardly congratulated myself upon my escape before he descended a few steps. This was much worse than ascending; if he fell, nothing could keep me from going over his head; but I remained till he put me down of his own accord. The poor fellow was wet with perspiration and trembled in every limb. Another stood ready to take me up, but I had had enough."

The trail became so rugged that even the mules now and then held back, afraid to go on. At one point, two of them fled into the woods rather than proceed.

Mico Mountain was nothing! This was a trail to end all trails. "It was the worst mountain I ever encountered," Stephens avowed, "in that or any other country, and, under our apprehension of the storm, I will venture to say that no travelers ever descended in less time."

It was also their last mountain. Very shortly they arrived at Palenque.

9

FORBIDDEN CITY

THE Indians stopped at the foot of a forested terrace and pointed, exclaiming, to the Palace.

Stephens spurred his horse forward.

"Through openings in the trees," as he described it, "we saw the front of a large building richly ornamented with stuccoed figures on the pilasters, curious and elegant, with trees growing close against it, their branches entering the doors; in style and effect it was unique, extraordinary, and mournfully beautiful.

"We tied our mules to the trees, ascended a flight of stone steps forced apart and thrown down by trees, and entered the palace. For a few moments we ranged along the corridor and into the courtyard, and after the first gaze of eager curiosity was over, went back to the entrance.

"Standing in the doorway, we fired a *feu-de-joie* of four rounds each, using up the last charge of our firearms. But for this way of giving vent to our satisfaction we should have made the roof of the old palace ring with a hurrah.

"It was intended, too, for effect upon the Indians, who had probably never heard such a cannonade before, and who, almost like their ancestors in the time of Cortéz, regarded our weapons as instruments which spit lightning. They would, we knew, make such a report in the village as would keep any of their respectable friends from paying us a visit at night."

After war, and hunger, and mountain trails, after a long and tiring journey through the wilds of Guatemala and southern Mexico, they had arrived at Palenque. Their first glance told them that it had been worth the trouble.

A dense forest of giant trees lay in all directions; how much of Palenque these trees concealed Stephens had no idea. The "palace" in which they took their abode rose out of the forest, or more correctly—since trees grew over the ruins—the palace rose *with* the forest. The Mexicans called it *El Palacio,* but no one can be sure that it was a palace occupied by Maya kings.

This main building contained fourteen doorways, and altogether measured 228 feet across the front. Columns supporting the roof were ornamented with bas-relief figures of excellent artistic quality. In the faces and elongated

General view of the ruins of Palenque, taken in 1963. Left of center is the Palace, where Stephens and his men stayed. The large temple at the right is the Temple of the Inscriptions, where Dr. Alberto Ruz discovered the burial chamber (see page 121)

Casa No. 1 at Palenque

heads, Stephens saw a strange race of people, Mayas who used to flatten and lengthen their babies' heads as a sign of beauty—or perhaps nobility. It was not a unique trait. He compared this to the habits of the Choctaw and Flathead Indians of his own country.

So excellent were the bas-reliefs that every detail of the superbly fashioned dress and ornamentation could be discerned. Catherwood must get his pencil busy copying these!

Immediately, they started in. As at Copán, Stephens and the workmen began to clear away trees, and Catherwood set up his easel. One glance told them that they couldn't draw or describe it all. The palace was enormous. Parallel corridors, in one of which they set up housekeeping, ran along all four sides, each some two hundred feet long. The plastered walls were almost twice as high as a man and,

here and there, they found the stucco covering painted
with red, blue, yellow, black, or white.

Stone steps led into broad courtyards, which had to be
cleared of trees. Once this was done, the explorers could
judge the magnificence of the art work. Carvings everywhere! Figures ten feet tall . . . life-sized jaguars, their
flattened backs apparently used as seats, perhaps as thrones
. . . murals depicting the lives and strange adventures of
the people . . . inscriptions adorning the walls . . . richly
engraved tablets . . . and fine profiles of the human face.

The buildings themselves were not as large as Stephens
and Catherwood had found elsewhere in the Maya Empire,
but the scenery was more spectacular. Palenque had been
built in the foothills of a great range in the province of
Chiapas, with steep mountains rising behind, mountains
that Stephens and his friends had painfully traveled
through. Below rolled a rich and attractive plain where
today are peaceful farms.

Stephens could see no other buildings from the palace.
But he knew they were there among the trees. Peering
into the jungle and cutting a short way through it, he found
other structures, hidden under the canopy of leaves and
even under the roots of trees. More treasures—art treasures
—more buildings elaborately ornamented, more of everything! There seemed to be no limit to the persistence and
skill of the ancient Mayas.

One stone tablet, nine feet wide and eight feet high,
set in a wall, was to Stephens the most perfect and interesting object at Palenque. Besides its ceremonial figures
of men standing on men, there were rows of completely un-
readable hieroglyphics.

If Palenque was not large as a city, it was a major center
of art and architecture. "Here were the remains of a cultivated, polished, and peculiar people," Stephens wrote,
"who had passed through all the stages incident to the rise

Tablet on back wall of altar, Casa No. 3 at Palenque

and fall of nations, had reached their golden age, and had perished, entirely unknown. The links connecting them with the human family were severed and lost; these were the only memorials of their footsteps upon earth.

"We lived in the ruined palace of their kings; we went up to their desolate temples and fallen altars; and wherever we moved we saw evidences of their taste, their skill in arts, their wealth and power. In the midst of desolation and ruin we looked back to the past, cleared away the gloomy forest, and fancied every building perfect, with its terraces and pyramids, its sculptured and painted ornaments, grand, lofty, and imposing, and overlooking an immense inhabited plain.

"We called back into life the strange people who gazed at us in sadness from the walls; pictured them, in fanciful costumes and adorned with plumes of feathers, ascending the terraces of the palace and the steps leading to the temples. . . . In the romance of the world's history nothing ever impressed me more forcibly than the spectacle of this once great and lovely city, overturned, desolate, and lost. . . ."

Had they been able to clear off all the trees and haul away some of the centuries' accumulation of fallen stones and rubbish, Stephens, Catherwood, and Pawling would have made some astonishing discoveries. Since the time of their visit, Palenque has been further explored and studied, and modern archeologists agree with Stephens that the palace buildings are outstanding among Maya ruins. High square towers and underground chambers and passages make the site unique.

Thanks to an excellent fine-grained limestone here, sculpture and stucco work reached an exceptional degree of development. The limestone was easily carved. It was strong and held its shape without splitting off or crumbling beneath the sculptor's tools. The temple tablets that Stephens marveled at are now considered masterpieces—the finest, most delicate, Maya artwork known.

Inscriptions have been found in more than ninety Maya sites, but the best are at Palenque. Stephens saw their resemblance to those of Copán and Quiriguá and this led him to believe that the region between these ruins was once occupied by a single race. But he had no way of knowing what the writings stood for, and therefore had no inkling of the age of these ruins.

Long after Stephens' time, archeologists discovered that the original monuments had been erected as early as A.D. 514. Great sculptured and architectural works were under way a century later, not only in Palenque but in the Maya centers of Yaxchilan and Piedras Negras, to the southeast in the Usumacinta River valley of Mexico and Guatemala. These sites reached their peak of occupation about the year A.D. 790. Then something happened. Construction ceased. The art work stopped. No more was stucco applied to the buildings, or walls and columns carved. No more were blocks of limestone carried in from quarries. No more were tablets engraved with intricate writings.

By A.D. 900, the buildings lay deserted, falling into ruin.

For centuries, Palenque was little touched by the superstitious descendants of the ancient builders. Then in 1750, two centuries after the coming of the Europeans, a party of Spaniards exploring the interior of Mexico came upon the ruins.

Word traveled fast. Count Jean Frédéric Waldeck, a Frenchman, came to Palenque in 1832 and stayed two years, drawing plans of the buildings and copying the Maya artwork. But Waldeck's drawings were not as faithful as they could have been; they contained too many of his own inventions. It was left to Catherwood to bring the real and true Palenque to the world. And he did it as only Frederick Catherwood could.

What no one could be sure of, among such marvelous ruins, was whether the Mayas had ever used these temples for burial. Had the ancients ever interred their greatest chiefs or warriors or priests beneath these hallowed halls?

It was a question that must have burned in the mind of every archeologist after Stephens. Somewhere under the dozens of rubble-covered mounds of Palenque might be an elaborate burial place—or at least a clue to one. The palace had crumbled in places to reveal some hidden underground passages sixty-five feet long. Were there tombs as well?

Not until after 1923, when the government began in earnest to excavate and restore the ruins, was the question answered by Alberto Ruz, a Mexican archeologist.

Digging beneath the Temple of the Inscriptions—where

Dr. Alberto Ruz

Stephens had found the huge wall tablet—Ruz discovered, in 1949, a narrow passageway completely filled with rubble. Taking out some of this, he found stone steps that were covered with stucco.

A stairway down! Nothing quite like it had ever been found in a Maya ruin.

But what a job digging it out! Heavy stones were raised by ropes and pulleys; clouds of dust caused Ruz's men to choke and cough; a whole summer's work was required to expose the first twenty-three steps. Then work had to stop. Heavy rains—like those Stephens had known so well—made life at Palenque unbearable.

Next season, Ruz came to rocks cemented tightly in the passageway. These had to be broken before they could be removed—a slow and vexing job. Another season passed, and still there was not a clue as to why this passage existed or why it had been filled and sealed with such determination.

When still another season passed, Ruz had gotten down to only seventy feet. It was discouraging. There were no inscriptions on the walls of the passage, no glyphs, no carvings, no sculpture, not even any of the bas-relief for which Palenque is so famous. Tons of debris had been lifted out—and the stairs continued downward.

In 1952, the workers broke through a wall of cemented rock and found a square stone box containing highly polished ornaments of jade, two painted ceramic plates, and a half-inch pearl. An offering?

Ahead lay a cemented wall that was twelve feet thick. Plunging to work eagerly, they found this wall extremely hard to cut through, as if they were entering a vault.

In truth, they were. For in the next chamber they beheld a masonry box containing six human skeletons. Was it the family of some great ruler, killed so that their spirits could go with his to the afterworld?

Stephens would have been beside himself with anticipation if he could have been at Ruz's side.

At last the men cut through a final wall into a darkened crypt and breathlessly held up their lights to see by.

It was a magic room from a forgotten civilization. Stalactites hung like curtains, glistening in the light. On the walls were stucco figures in low relief. In the center of the chamber lay a giant slab of stone, twelve feet long and seven wide, on which were carved a man in elaborate headdress, two-headed serpents, plumed birds, and bordering glyphs. The slab must have weighed five tons.

Testing carefully, Ruz detected the presence of a hollow space beneath. Something was under the slab. The cover would have to be raised, no matter how heavy. But they

Temple of Inscriptions, Palenque, as it looked about two years after Dr. Ruz discovered its burial chamber

had to do it carefully, in order not to crack or break it, for the stone was a masterpiece.

Jacking up the sides of the slab, inch by inch, slipping boards underneath so that the stone would not fall, they raised it slowly and with utmost care.

Ruz could scarcely wait. They had raised the slab but fifteen inches, when he stopped the work and squeezed beneath.

"My first impression," he wrote, "was that of a mosaic of green, red, and white. Then it resolved itself into details—green jade ornaments, red painted teeth and bones, and fragments of a mask. I was gazing at the death face of him for whom all this stupendous work—the crypt, the sculpture, the stairway, the great pyramid with its crowning temple—

Burial chamber tomb discovered by Dr. Alberto Ruz, beneath the Temple of the Inscriptions. The large decorated stone in the lower half of the picture is a large slab that covered a crypt in which were the remains of some important ancient Mayan. Below is a detail of the carving on the slab

had been built. . . . This, then, was a sarcophagus, the first ever found in a Mayan pyramid."

When finally the lid of the ancient coffin was removed, they saw the skeleton of a Maya chief who had been between forty and fifty years old. His teeth were painted red. His body was adorned with rings, bracelets, ear ornaments, and figurines—literally covered with jade.

We need but little imagination to guess how Stephens would have felt had he discovered all this in 1840.

It was just such a prospect that kept him and Catherwood and Pawling in Palenque, clearing, digging, and drawing, despite the rains.

And despite the mosquitoes. These creatures drove away all rest, said Stephens, and at times were beyond endurance. The slightest part of the body exposed was bitten, and in the morning the faces of the men were painfully blotched. Worse yet were tiny creatures that bored into human flesh and laid their eggs. Stephens got such a serious foot infection this way that he had to be carried from the ruins to the nearest village for help.

In the incessant rains, the guns and pistols rusted and everything became soggy and mildewed—clothes, equipment, food, and drawing materials. Of more concern to Stephens was Catherwood's health. During their months of hardship and privation, the artist had grown unusually pale and thin. He was lame from bites of insects. His face was swollen. His left arm dangled weakly on account of aches and pains.

As a matter of fact, all the men were pushing to the limit of their endurance, and Stephens knew it.

"Every day our residence became more wet and uncomfortable," he wrote. "On Thursday, the thirtieth of May, the storm opened with a whirlwind. At night the crash of falling trees rang through the forest, rain fell in deluges, the roaring of thunder was terrific, and as we lay looking out, the aspect of the ruined palace, lighted by the glare of lightning such as I never saw in this country, was awfully grand; in fact, there was too much of the sublime and terrible.

"The storm threatened the very existence of the building; and, knowing the tottering state of the walls, for some moments we had apprehensions lest the whole should fall and crush us. In the morning the courtyard and the ground below the palace were flooded, and by this time the whole front was so wet that we were obliged to desert it and move to the other side of the corridor.

"Even here we were not much better off; but we remained until Mr. Catherwood had finished his last drawing; and on Saturday, the first of June, like rats leaving a sinking ship, we broke up and left the ruins."

With Catherwood on the verge of collapse and unable to ride, and with the muddy roads all but impassable, they decided to go by canoe, down the Río Usumacinta to the Gulf of Mexico, thence to Yucatán, and thence to New York—if necessary.

Before leaving, Stephens had one painful duty: to leave behind his faithful mule.

"He had carried me more than two thousand miles over the worst roads that mule ever traveled. He stood tied to the door of the convent and saw the luggage, even his own saddle, carried away by hand; he seemed to have a presentiment that something unusual was going on. I had often been solicited to sell him, but no money could have tempted me. He was in poorer condition than when we reached Palenque. Deprived of corn and exposed to the dreadful rains, he was worse than when worked hard and fed well every day; in his drooping state he seemed to reproach me for going away and leaving him forlorn.

"I threw my arms around his neck; his eyes had a mournful expression, and at that moment he forgot the angry prick of the spur. I laid aside the memory of a toss from his back and ineffectual attempts to repeat it, and we remembered only mutual kind offices and good-fellowship.

"Tried and faithful companion, where are you now? I left him, with two others . . . to recover from the debilitating influence of the early rains, and to roam on rich pasture grounds, untouched by bridle or spur, until I should return to mount him again."

Down the Usumacinta they went. Shortly after reaching the Gulf of Mexico at the village of Carmen, they boarded the brig *Gabrielacho*. Here Pawling left them. In order to earn money for his passage to the United States of America, which he still desperately wanted, he agreed to return to Palenque to make plaster casts of the tablets and other objects of Maya art so that they could be placed on display. Stephens intended to establish a Museum of American Antiquities, presumably in New York City.

He was never able to do this, however, on account of the difficulties of getting valuable objects out of the various countries. Nor could he have guessed, as they said good-by, that Pawling would make some splendid plaster casts of Palenque sculpture—only to have the Mexican authorities demand so high a price for taking the copies out of the country that the deal fell through. Pawling left Palenque in 1840; whether or not he ever got to the U.S.A., Stephens does not say.

Arriving at Mérida, Stephens and Catherwood went to the ruins of Uxmal, staying at a *hacienda* there, but they ran into serious trouble. "We passed a most interesting and laborious day," Stephens wrote, "and at evening returned to the hacienda to mature our plans for a thorough exploration. Unfortunately, during the night Mr. Catherwood, affected, I believe, by the immensity of the work, had a violent attack of fever, which continued upon him in the morning with a prospect of serious illness."

And later: "The hacienda was unhealthy at this season; the great troughs and tanks of water around the house were green and, with the regular afternoon rains, they induced fatal fevers. Mr. Catherwood's constitution was already severely shattered. Indeed, I became alarmed and considered it indispensable for him to leave the hacienda and, if possible, the country altogether. To carry out my other plans, we intended at all events to return. We made a calculation that, by setting out the next morning, we could reach the Spanish brig in time to embark for Havana, and in ten minutes' consulation we determined to break up and go home.

"Immediately we communicated our purpose to the major-domo, who ascended the belfry of the church and called a coach to be ready at two o'clock the next morning."

Stephens knew he would be back.

10

FIESTA IN YUCATAN

A gay company gathered in the plaza of Ticul. Dusk had fallen, and the glow of sunset lingered to silhouette the towering village church. Dogs barked, and children ran in and out of the bullring. Crowds of people were laughing and talking beneath a blaze of lanterns, candles, and torches. Under an enclosed arbor at one side, where there was a concrete floor for dancing, music could be heard.

The fiesta had begun. It was the *baile de las mestizas,* the maiden's ball.

Villagers, *vaqueros* (cowboys), and farmers from miles around had come to Ticul for the festival, traveling by foot, or cart, or horseback, down the dusty roads and across the fields of Yucatán.

The *vaqueros,* like all young cowboys of Mexico, loved the fiesta, and were dressed gaily for it: narrow-brimmed straw hats rolled up at the sides and trimmed with gold cord and tassels, pink-striped shirts and trousers, and shoes of yellow buckskin. What pretty *mestiza* could resist them?

The *mestizas* themselves, seated in chairs along the side of the arbor, were fitted out in costumes to entrance the *vaqueros* in return. The girls wore loose, red-bordered shirts of white that contrasted with their brown-skinned shoulders. They also wore men's black *sombreros* (hats), and necklaces and bracelets of gold. Over their shoulders were blue woven scarves.

And there on the other side, as kingly as you please, sat the bearded, red-haired New Yorker who, with his friends, had just come back from *El Norte* to resume his studies of the ancient ruins.

He had come through here the year before to study the ruins. At that time he had been on his way from Palenque to New York. The people of Yucatán had come to know him well. He liked them, and they him. Now he had come back to them. They must have known that he could not stay away long!

There was a debonair, almost mischievous, smile on John Lloyd Stephens' face. He sat in an armchair, cigar in hand, puffing with pleasure. The hard work of the day at the ruins, the mosquitoes, the dust, thirst, heat—all were forgotten now in the presence of the singing, the dancing, the smells of the village, the sweat of cowboys, the perfume of the *mestizas*.

To be back, to be exploring the ruins again, to be attending the fiesta—this was what he had waited for!

It seemed only yesterday that they had floated in their canoes down the Usumacinta River. They had gotten Catherwood to New York in time to prevent the artist's complete collapse. And while Catherwood had been recovering, Stephens had gathered together his soiled, crumpled, rain-soaked notebooks and had written.

For nearly a year, the celebrated author of *Incidents of Travel in Arabia* and other parts of the world worked on a new book, *Incidents of Travel in Central America, Chiapas, & Yucatán.* In it were exciting tales of discovery, adventure, war, beauty, hardships, Indians. And if anyone doubted the marvels of the Maya ruins, engravings from Catherwood's drawings resolved those doubts. The book was an instant success. Praise poured in from readers everywhere, catapulting Stephens to eminence in the literary world.

Besides, there were enough political battles, elections,

and intrigues in the contemporary world to satisfy his taste
—in fact, more than enough.

Stephens had reported to the Secretary of State, John
Forsyth, on his mission to Central America. The Secretary
had hoped that Stephens would bring back a treaty of
peace and commerce between the United States of America
and the United States of Central America. Van Buren
needed this sort of successful enterprise to help him get
reelected—for he was having political troubles. But it was
not to be; Stephens brought only reports of Maya ruins.

Van Buren was defeated, anyway, and William Henry
Harrison—famed as a general in the War of 1812—became
President. Harrison appointed Daniel Webster, the cele-
brated statesman and orator, as his Secretary of State.
Stephens and Webster met and talked about the Maya ruins.
Webster could appreciate the importance of Stephens' dis-
coveries. He even offered Stephens a position as Secretary
of the United States Legation in Mexico.

But then William Henry Harrison died, and the Vice-
President John Tyler, became President. The situation was
confused. With the changes of government, Stephens' future
would be anything but certain. He finally declined the offer.

Besides, nowhere in New York or Washington could he
smell the dank and musty odors of the ancient Maya ruins,
or the hot, lime-smelling sidewalks of villages in Yucatán.
Nowhere were there dusty streets that rang with the happy
shouts of the *vaqueros* or the familiar laughter of the *mestizas*.

The lure of the Tropics had beckoned, and now he was
back. Catherwood had recovered his health and had come
back, too, and this time Stephens had engaged a young
doctor, Samuel Cabot. Cabot was well-built, athletic, blue-
eyed, slightly taller than Stephens. He had been a champion
boxer at Harvard. His skill as a doctor made him very popu-

lar in Yucatán, but he could hardly cope with all the ills and injuries that he saw—or that were brought to him.

Dr. Cabot was a naturalist too. He would often plunge into the jungle with his gun in search of new species of birds. This was also a good way to discover new ruins, and he did. But mostly his intent was to preserve the skins and feathers of birds so that these could be taken back to museums and universities for study.

Vaqueros and *mestizas* began to dance, gracefully swinging their bodies, flinging their arms joyously, snapping their fingers, and laughing—always laughing. Their eyes sparkled in the light of the candles and lanterns. Stephens was caught up fully with the spirit of the festival, savoring every sight and sound as the evening wore on, and on.

On this glorious night in Ticul, Catherwood and Cabot had remained at camp. In the excitement of the fiesta Stephens quite forgot about them.

Late into the night the merriment continued and started again the next morning, with all the participants as bright-eyed as ever. With the coming of daylight, rocket explosions and ringing bells announced the resumption of the festival. After Mass in the church came cattle-roping in the plaza. *Vaqueros* young and old galloped into the arena, swung their lassos high overhead, and sped after bulls in all directions. Women and children squealed in fright and delight and scampered out of the way.

"One horse fell and hurt his rider," Stephens reported, "but there were no necks broken."

That over, the dances of the day began. As the hot rays of the sun poured into the plaza, *vaqueros* escorted their *mestizas* to the arbor. It didn't seem possible, Stephens thought, but the maidens appeared to be even prettier.

Indians in cotton shirts and breeches, either barefoot

or wearing sandals, crowded in as well, so that soon there was hardly room under the arbor to stand or sit.

Noisily bossing the crowd were assorted village officials, in loose-fitting dirty shirts, breeches, wide-brimmed hats, and sandals. Each carried a whip of eight or ten lashes, with which he playfully inflicted punishment. Everyone was in a state of laughter and confusion.

Suddenly a fat man appeared in the doorway—no doubt some high official of the village, Stephens thought. The officers quickly cleared an opening in the crowd, then dashed across the floor, seized the fat man, pulled him to the center of the floor and, with groans of effort, lifted him up and placed him on the shoulders of a *vaquero.*

Once this was done, they taunted and pulled at him, and jeered and made funny faces that sent the watching multitude into roars of laughter. The fat man, and the *vaquero* carrying him, laughed so hard they almost fell to the floor together.

At this point, the officials turned and walked toward Stephens. One in the lead raised his lash and spoke to Stephens in a loud voice as he came.

"His eyes, sparkling with frolic and mischief, fastened upon mine," Stephens later wrote. "The crowd followed, and I was a little afraid of an attempt to hoist me too on the shoulders of a *vaquero;* but all at once he stopped short, and, unexpectedly changing his language, opened upon me with a loud harangue in Maya.

"All knew that I did not understand a word he said, and the laugh was strong against me. I was a little annoyed at being made such a mark, but . . . I answered him with an English oration.

"The effect was instantaneous. He had never before heard a language that he could not understand, bent his ear earnestly, as if by close attention he could catch the

meaning, and looked up with an air of real perplexity that
turned the laugh completely against him. He began again,
and I answered with a stanza of Greek poetry, which had
hung by me in some unaccountable way; this, again, completely silenced him. He put his arms around my neck,
called me '*amigo*,' and made a covenant not to speak in any
language but Castilian."

The music commenced, and out came the *mestizas* to
dance. One of them especially caught Stephens' attention.
He described her as "not more than fifteen, delicate and
fragile, with eyes so soft and dovelike that it was impossible
to look upon them without a feeling of tenderness. She
seemed sent into the world to be cherished and cared for
and closeted like the finest china, the very emblem of purity,
innocence, and loveliness."

In the midst of the proceedings, a village official rose,
pushed a *vaquero* away from one of the *mestizas*, laid a
shawl at her feet, and began to dance around her. She did
not smile or even look at him.

Furiously he danced, up and down, around and around.
She ignored him. He tore off his sash and flung it at her
feet. She turned her head in mock disdain. But with the
sash flung away, his breeches began to fall. Desperately
he clutched them to hold them up, still dancing furiously.
The crowd roared.

Amid gales of laughter, the dance ended. The lady
bowed and took her seat.

Suddenly, the dancer turned to Stephens, calling out
in Spanish; "*Amigo!* Are there girls like that in your country?"

The crowd burst out in an explosion of laughter. Stephens does not say what his reply was.

"Well," said the dancer, "would you like to take her
home with you?"

Then he thought better of that idea and said, "No! I cannot spare that one. But, *amigo,* take your choice of the others!"

Everybody joined in the dancing, and soon they were all singing together a cowboy song, half in Spanish, half in Mayan.

At noon, the merriment abated a trifle for lunch, and a great clay barrel filled with fried black beans was brought in. After this came a barrel containing eggs and meat. Then *tortillas*—"a mountain of *tortillas*" Stephens said—served by the *mestizas.* After the food, the dancing resumed.

Stephens could have spent all day there, and the night as well, but alas—"At two o'clock, to my great regret, the ball of *las mestizas* broke up. It was something entirely new, and remains engraven on my mind as the best of the village balls."

Ticul became quiet once again. The *mestizas* began to withdraw. The *vaqueros* settled down in the shade for a nap, and to escape the brutal heat of the afternoon sun. As for the New Yorker, it was time for him to go back to the ruins, to see how Catherwood and Cabot were getting along.

Stephens walked to his horse. Yes, it was good to be back. It was good to be among these happy, friendly, simple people of Yucatán. He mounted, tipped his hat to the *mestizas,* and smiled at the *vaqueros.*

Then he turned down the dusty street and rode out of town.

11

TEMPLES OF THE PAST

THE path led through what Stephens called "a noble piece of woods." He recalled the great astonishment he had felt when first he stepped out of the woods and viewed the ruins. The other sites—Copán, Palenque, all of them—had been covered with vegetation. What a glorious open sight this was, the view uncluttered by trees, vines, and shrubs: carved stone buildings of great dimensions sprawling on man-made terraces; pyramidal structures; oval mounds, and mountains of ruins.

Not one word about Uxmal had Stephens seen in any history book. Two years before, Count Waldeck had published in Paris a book on the archeological ruins of Yucatán, but that was imperfect because at that time the ruins were partly covered with trees. Now the trees had been cleared away, and Stephens and Catherwood had unobstructed views for their work.

Moving out onto open ground toward the nearest ruin, Stephens was again tormented by questions crowding through his mind. Who built these imposing structures? Why here? When and why were they abandoned? Uxmal had not been the original name of this city, he was certain of that. Uxmal was simply the name of a Mexican *hacienda* nearby. What the ancient inhabitants had called their city no one knew.

With his Indian guides and workers, Stephens walked up the slope to a towering oval mound, with a temple perched on top. House of the Dwarf, the Indians called it, and in their minds were legends and superstitions about these ruins. They would not come near the buildings at night.

The mound on which the House of the Dwarf was situated had steeply pitching sides, with more than a hundred steps so vertical and in such a state of disrepair that great care had to be used in ascending and descending, lest a climber tumble and break his neck.

The structure on top contained three narrow chambers nine feet wide, the two on the end being eighteen feet long, and the one in the center thirty-four feet. Like most Maya buildings, it had no windows. For doors there were simply openings at each end.

What caught Stephens' eye at once was a cornice of richly sculptured ornaments above the doors. This cornice extended all around the building. Never had he seen anything like it—not in Copán, not in Palenque, not even in the ruined cities between Palenque and here. "The designs were strange and incomprehensible," he wrote, "very elaborate, sometimes grotesque, but often simple, tasteful, and beautiful."

The whole effect, to Stephens, was one of grandness and curiosity. The designs had a strangeness that he could not explain: square and diamond shapes, busts of human beings, heads of jaguars, leaves, flowers. There were no single tablets or separate stones with their own stories of the kind he had seen so often south of here. Instead, some master architect had worked each stone and slab into a grand design that ran the length of the building.

From where he stood on the *Casa del Enano,* or House of the Dwarf, he could see the Yucatán jungle spreading like a fluffy carpet in all directions. The *hacienda,* in which he had taken lodging, lay to the north.

Below and to the west lay the *Casa de las Monjas,* House of the Nuns, a broad, low collection of buildings which he calculated to be 250 feet square. It sat on a terrace, fifteen

Casa del Enano (House of the Dwarf), Uxmal: (Above) as drawn by Catherwood; (Below) as it is today (Photo by Suttons). "In attempting a description of these ruins, so vast a work rises up before me that I am at a loss to begin. . . . The first object that arrests the eye on emerging from the forest {is} this lofty structure. . . . The elevation on which it stands is built up solid from the plain, entirely artificial. Its form is not pyramidal, but oblong and rounding . . ."

Interior courtyard, Casa de las Monjas (House of the Nuns), Uxmal, today. "The principal entrance is by a large doorway into a beautiful patio or courtyard, grass-

feet high, and was sculptured with the same richness and brilliance of design as the House of the Dwarf.

As he clambered down the broken and dangerous stairway from the House of the Dwarf, Stephens wondered, as he had so often in Mexico and Guatemala, what manner of people could have achieved so advanced a state of art and architecture.

From the fallen slabs along the wall of the House of the Nuns he looked to the south, where lay ruin after ruin, mound after mound. Prominently and majestically in the distance rose the greatest masterpiece, the *Casa del Gobernador*, House of the Governor, which he later measured and found to be 320 feet long. In Stephens' opinion it was "the grandest in position, the most stately in architecture and proportions, and the most perfect in preservation of all the structures remaining at Uxmal."

grown but clear of trees, and the whole of the inner fa-
cade is ornamented more richly and elaborately than the
outside, and is in a more perfect state of preservation."

It stood on the topmost of three specially constructed
terraces, the lowest of which measured 600 feet in length,
and all of which must have required a prodigious amount
of work to build. Like the other buildings, the *Casa del
Gobernador* had been constructed of stone, and had been
far better preserved than the ruins of Palenque, probably
on account of a relatively drier climate here. It was richly
carved and ornamented in the fashion of the House of the
Dwarf and the House of the Nuns, the mosaics extending
the entire length of the building. No work of savages this,
he thought. Here lived a people not of Greece or of Egypt.
A civilization had risen, flourished, and perished on its own,
here in the Western Hemisphere.

Bats flew out as the explorers went in. Though some of
the doorways of the *Casa del Gobernador* had collapsed,
and piles of fallen stone lay here and there, the rooms were

still in reasonably good condition. They did not leak, at any rate, so Stephens and Catherwood took up their abode in this building in order to be, literally, on top of their work.

Inside, where the gloom of darkness veiled their view, they found a floor composed of smooth square stones, and walls of square-cut blocks that had been polished by Indian hands no telling how many centuries before. With the passage of time, the floor was slowly crumbling and now lay broken beneath their feet.

Remarkable as the architecture was, Stephens saw not a single arch—only corbelled vaults that formed triangular

Designs on wall of courtyard at Casa de las Monjas. "It is built entirely of cut stone, and the whole exterior is filled with the same rich, elaborate, and incomprehensible sculptured ornaments."

*East facade, Casa del Gobernador, Uxmal, showing two-headed jaguar
sculpture on platform in front of building. "On digging down to a
depth of three or four feet, a sculptured monument was discovered.
. . . It was found standing on its feet . . . carved out of a single
block of stone. . . . It seems intended to represent a double-headed
cat or lynx."*

openings. The Mayas apparently never discovered the simple arch with its fitted keystone.

Designs on the face of the *Casa del Gobernador* so fascinated Catherwood that he erected a ladder in order to copy them as closely and exactly as they had been fashioned by the ancient sculptors.

Nor was the *Casa del Gobernador* the last of Uxmal's buildings. Far from it. Below one corner rose a temple ornamented all around with sculptured turtles. *Casa de Tortugas*, the Mexicans called it, House of Turtles. To the west were other buildings.

Exultant, fired with the fever of discovery, Stephens clambered over one ruined building after another, searching, probing, climbing on terraces that lifted these regal structures out of the sprawling jungle. Had anyone pointed out the dangers of these exploration, he would have smiled and walked away. In almost every case the decay of time was evident. Roofs had collapsed, filling ancient rooms with rubble. Doorways, precariously supported by lintels, gave promise of falling at any moment. In one place he walked on ground that sounded hollow to the step and, sure enough, found openings that led to cave-like rooms below.

But no "idols," no stelae, no tablets as meticulously carved as those at Palenque. Something had changed. Uxmal was different. Were these temples really built and occupied by the same kind of people who had built Copán and Palenque?

Of all the jobs Stephens had at Uxmal, that of supervising the Indians was to him the most tedious and time-consuming. The Indian workmen moved sluggishly in this hot and humid climate. They did not seem to share his interest in the ruins. Perhaps they should have; it was likely enough their own ancestors who had built Uxmal and performed religious ceremonies here. In fact, when burials were

(Left) Casa de Tortugas (House of Turtles); (Right) Casa de las Monjas, with ball court below it. ". . . on a line with the door of the convent, is another building, on a lower foundation, of the same general character, called Casa de Tortugas, from sculptured

unearthed, the Indians would exclaim, "These are the bones of our kinsmen."

Difficulties or not, Stephens was glad to be back. "The ruins of Uxmal presented themselves to me as a home," he said, "and I looked upon them with more interest than before. I had found the wrecks of cities scattered more numerously than I expected, but they were all so shattered that no voice of instruction issued from them; here they still stood, tottering and crumbling, but living memorials, more worthy than ever of investigation and study. . . ."

Each night they lighted a fire in the corner of their room to drive out the dreaded mosquitoes. And often Stephens' attacks of malaria returned. One day he finished his work in such a state of weakness that his legs would hardly support him. He dragged himself to their room in the *Casa del Gobernador*. His throat was dry, but no amount of water seemed to slake his thirst. He fell into his hammock, burning with fever.

For days the fierce attacks of malaria came and went

turtles over the doorway. This building had in several places huge cracks, as if it had been shaken by an earthquake. It stands nearly in the center of the ruins, and the top commands a view all round of singular but wrecked magnificence."

and at length grew so bad that he had to be carried nine miles away to a village church for rest and treatment.

Some days later, while recuperating, he started on a stroll with the village priest, or *cura.* "We had gone but a short distance," he wrote, "when an Indian came running after us to inform us that another of the *caballeros* had arrived sick from the ruins. We hurried back and found Doctor Cabot lying . . . at the door. . . .

"I was startled by the extraordinary change a few days had made in his appearance. His face was flushed, his eyes were wild, his figure lank, and he had not strength to support himself, but pitched against me, who could barely keep myself up, and both nearly came down together. He had been attacked the day after I left, and the fever had been upon him, with but little intermission, ever since. All night and all the two ensuing days, it continued rising and decreasing, but never leaving him. It was attended with constant restlessness and delirium, so that he was hardly in bed before he was up again, pitching about the room."

Once well again, however, sitting at the ruins in the cool of the evening, Stephens could forget his troubles. The beauty of Uxmal, and of the country, never escaped him. "Flames lighted up the facade of the great palace," he wrote one night, "and when they died away, the full moon broke upon it, mellowing its rents and fissures and presenting a scene mournfully beautiful."

He had himself lowered down on a rope so that he could crawl around on hands and knees and explore the hidden chambers beneath the ground. He never knew when he would run into a nest of hornets, which had happened once, and be repeatedly stung while he dangled almost helplessly at the end of the rope. Nor could he take every possible precaution against poisonous snakes and scorpions. Perhaps the only effective defense against these would have been to stay at home in the first place.

Detail of Casa del Gobernador, showing corbelled vault at right. "Every ornament or combination is made up of separate stones, each of which had carved on it part of the subject, and was then set in its place in the wall. Each stone by itself is an unmeaning fractional portion, but, placed by the side of others makes part of a whole, which without it would be incomplete."

Try as they might to keep supplied with water, thirst plagued them. The *hacienda* from which they got their food and water was more than a mile distant. They attempted to store some water at the *Casa del Gobernador,* but this was not easy. Their supply very often gave out. The burning sun and searing heat drew from them quantities of sweat and, when they arrived at their rooms with throats all parched, they sometimes had to wait until an Indian could go to the *hacienda* for water.

This raised the question of how the ancient Indians had gotten *their* water. Stephens had seen neither wells, nor streams, nor springs that could have supplied the number of people that must have once lived here and in the neighboring forest.

But one day, looking out from the top of the House of

the Dwarf, he saw a pond about one and a half miles away. After Indians had cleared a path through the forest, Stephens made his way to it, discovering a shallow expanse of excellent water.

To his surprise, the Indians told him that these ponds lay in basins scooped out by human hands. Sure enough, when the water was low, stone embankments could be seen. The ancient people of Uxmal must have scoured the basin out, dug wells, or cisterns, in the bottom, and lined the whole with stone. If so, these ponds held water during drought, enough to tide the people over until a season of rain came again.

One day, while clearing a tall mound near the *Casa del Gobernador,* Stephens came upon an ornament that suggested a doorway beneath. Calling to the Indians, he bade them dig into the mound so as to open an entrance to whatever chamber lay below. He sent for Catherwood and Cabot so that they could all enter together and record the fabulous discoveries they were likely to make.

Naturally, the Indians dug too slowly for Stephens, and when the hole got deep, they refused to continue for fear of rocks sliding down upon them. This was too much.

"I threw myself into the hole," Stephens wrote, describing his state of frenzied expectation, "and commenced digging with all my strength. The stones went rolling and crashing down the side of the mound, striking against roots and tearing off branches. The perspiration rolled from me in a stream, but I was so completely carried away by the idea that had taken possession of me, so sure of entering some chamber that had been closed for ages, that I stopped at nothing. . . ."

But there was no opening. There was no doorway. There was no fabled chamber of a buried king. All they found was another solid wall.

It was this kind of hard work, this excitement, and this

disappointment that left Stephens nearly exhausted, too weak and debilitated to fight off attacks of malaria.

Yet the great sculpture, the painting (some of the original colors could still be seen), and the architecture kept him going, as had such things in Egypt. "Imagine what the effect must have been," he wrote, "when all this building was entire. . . . In its now desolate doorways stood noble Maya maidens, like the vestal virgins of the Romans, to cherish and keep alive the sacred fire burning in the temples."

The people of those ancient times still lived, through their engravings. Stephens had come upon evidence of gruesome sacrifices that must have been held here. He had read historians' accounts about Indian high priests and their broad flint knives. The persons to be sacrificed mounted the steps of the temples, were laid out on a stone altar, fitted with wooden collars, and held down by four priests who gripped their hands and feet. The high priest ripped open the breast and tore out the heart of the victim, holding it up as an offering to the sun, great giver of life.

Stephens wrote his own opinion about this practice. "In all the long catalogue of superstitious rites that darkens the page of man's history, I cannot imagine a picture more horribly exciting than that of the Indian priest, with his white dress and long hair clotted with gore, performing his murderous sacrifices at this lofty height, in full view of the people throughout the whole extent of the city."

12

CHICHEN ITZA

THEY were like names from another world—Labná, Sayil, Nohpat, Kabah, Xcoch, Kiuik, Chunhuhú. As a matter of fact, they did represent another world, for they were the names of Maya ruins. Stephens visited them all.

There were also nameless ruins—lone piles of fallen stone, mounds hidden by the jungle vegetation of Yucatán, dark caverns, and musty rooms. Curiosity drew the little party of explorers into tight and even dangerous places. They crawled with torches through tiny cavern passages, and after a day of that they were, as Stephens put it, dripping with sweat, black with smoke, and perishing with thirst.

This kind of hardship would have caused no trouble had not the attacks of malaria worsened. Once all three of them—Stephens, Catherwood, and Cabot—fell ill at the same time.

Too often the fatigue and excitement were more than Stephens could take. "My bones ached; a chill crept over me; I looked around for a soft stone to lie down upon; but the place was cold and damp, and rain was threatening. I saddled my horse, and when I mounted, I could hardly keep my seat. I had no spurs; my horse seemed to know my condition and went on a slow walk, nibbling at every bush. The fever came on, and I was obliged to dismount and lie down under a bush; but the *garrapatas* [ticks] drove me away."

They worked their way across Yucatán toward the east, exploring dark and silent chambers, many of which had, no doubt, never been seen by white men. One sentence in his journal summarizes the essence of Stephens' search for ruins and studies of the ancient Indians: "We were the first to throw open the portals of their grave, and they are now for the first time presented to the public."

Yet he could do little more about these lesser ruined cities and numerous mounds scattered over the peninsula than announce their existence. Catherwood made drawings of some of the more magnificent, such as Kabah. But all that Stephens could safely conclude was that there had been a grand and glorious civilization in this region. With each passing year the ruins were becoming more shapeless and overgrown.

The country through which they traveled seemed endlessly flat. They could see little of it through the trees, of course, but, when they mounted one of the high ruins that pierced the canopy of leaves, it was easy to scan the tropical terrain of Yucatán.

In all directions lay jungle, as far as the eye could see. Upward the clouds rose into a misty, pale blue sky. Only on occasion did those clouds build up into dramatic thunderheads. Then they would burst with lightning, thunder would crash and echo down among the trees, and heavy rain would plunge into the forest like a giant waterfall. After this, the jungle would be refreshed and cool again—at least for a while.

When at last they came to the "frontier," as Stephens called it, they looked to the south across the green wilderness that stretched toward the region of Lake Petén. There the Lacandones lived (and still do), a race of Indians as unknown and mysterious as the ancient cities supposed to exist in the same region.

Unexplored. Unknown. *Desconocido.* These were words very often heard. The Indians knew little or nothing, not even the whereabouts, of some of the ruined cities Stephens

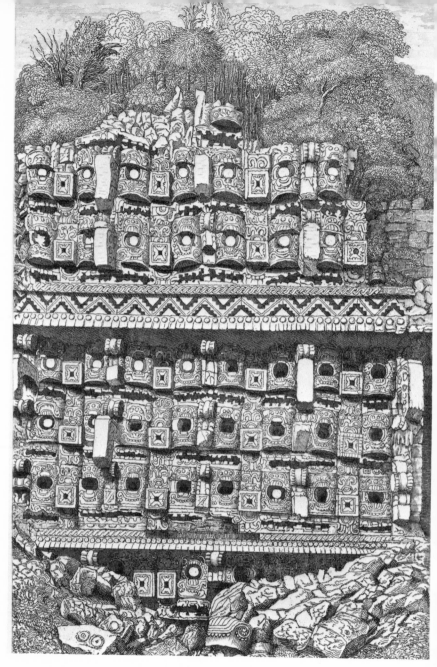

Detail of ornament, Casa No. 1, Kabah

discovered on this journey. The Spanish knew little more, which seemed surprising because the land had been theirs for three centuries.

A sailor who had been with Columbus was probably the first European to discover Yucatán, which the Maya themselves called *uluumil cutz yetel ceh*, land of the turkey and the deer. When the early Spanish asked them the name of their country, they misunderstood the question and replied, "*Ci uthan*," literally "you say so," meaning perhaps, "what did you say?" The Spaniards thought this reply denoted the name of the land, and through the years changed it to Yucatán.

Afterwards the Spanish flood of conquest began. The flood of blood also began, for when Hernandez de Córdoba and 110 soldiers from Cuba landed in Yucatán in 1517, they were ambushed by Indians who showered them with arrows. But arrows could hardly match the crossbows, swords, and firearms of the Spanish. In the aftermath, Mayas lay dead or dying across the battlefield.

Córdoba marched to the village of Kimpech, now Campeche, where he learned that the Mayas were on the move and had made sacrifices in a ceremony dedicated to his destruction.

Hearing this, he and his men withdrew and continued along the coast toward the west. They met and defeated more Mayas, but soon realized that their party was simply too small to last very long in the face of overwhelming numbers of Indians.

In their final battle, Córdoba and his soldiers were literally pushed into the sea. Sixty-two of his men were killed and nearly all were wounded two, three, or four times. Córdoba himself had twelve arrow wounds.

He returned to Cuba, and died ten days after arrival. His trip was disastrous, but it proved that the Mayas, however primitive, were a very tough breed of men.

The Mayas launched their arrows against the soldiers of Juan de Grijalva in 1518, but Grijalva got far enough along the coast to hear that magic word "Mexico." It was toward Mexico that the next expedition headed, commanded by an unknown Cuban official named Hernán Cortéz. This band of conquerors established a beachhead where the city of Veracruz now stands, fought its way inland, set tribe against tribe, took on Indian allies, climbed to the highlands of central Mexico, laid siege to the great stronghold of Montezuma, and in some of the bloodiest battles ever fought, wrested the country from the Indians.

This conquest of Mexico made Cortéz a hero. But it was not a complete conquest. There was still Yucatán.

Don Francisco de Montejo, one of Cortéz's captains who had earlier sailed with Grijalva, was granted the privilege of conquering Yucatán and for that purpose sailed from Spain in 1527.

He landed peacefully enough on the idyllic island of Cozumel, near the eastern shore of Yucatán. But the Indians were gathering for war, and Montejo readied his men for action. On the mainland he found thick woods that were nearly impenetrable and heat that was almost unbearable. The Spaniards met Mayas armed with arrows, flint-tipped lances, and primitive swords fashioned from wood that was as hard as iron.

"Viva España!" shouted the Spaniards, and the battles commenced. As usual, the Indians stood their ground, fighting bravely and desperately, but with vastly inferior weapons. They fell by the thousands.

Montejo got to Chichén Itzá, site of ancient Maya buildings, and there set up headquarters. Battle followed battle, and not only Mayas were killed ; the Spaniards suffered serious losses, too. Seeing that the Indians were massing to kill them, Montejo and his men managed—with a certain amount of luck—to escape to the coast. They apparently paid little attention to the Maya ruins. When they left, Chichén Itzá slumbered on, little known, and visited only by Indians, for nearly three centuries.

Montejo and his soldiers tried to reestablish a foothold in Yucatán, but its conquest was tougher than they had imagined. In 1535 they still had not succeeded and so, for the time being, gave up the effort.

Two years later they landed again, and again the Indians lay in wait. This time, as before, in repeated encounters, the Spaniards slaughtered Indians by the thousands. Arquebuses—the first hand guns—and crossbows mowed down the hapless Mayas in such heaps that the Spaniards could scarcely climb over their bodies to pursue the survivors.

Finally, some of the tribes—as if awestruck by the enormous power, the weapons, and the horses of the invaders—surrendered. A few even joined the Spaniards.

After this, the end was inevitable. The conquest of Yucatán was all but over. The Spaniards had won, and the land· was theirs. In 1542, just fifty years after Columbus first set sail across the ocean, the city of Mérida was founded.

On the afternoon of March 11, 1842, Stephens and his entourage arrived at the ruins of Chichén Itzá. They had learned of these ruins from a report that had appeared scarcely a year before. In fact, the ruins had been rediscovered by an explorer from the United States only two years earlier than that.

To Stephens, this was a moment to be remembered. Even after all that he and Catherwood had seen on their journeys, Chichén Itzá excited in them new and profound "emotions of wonder."

It is not surprising that it should have. As they approached, they saw through the trees a temple of white limestone rising above the jungle. The pyramid-like platform on which it rested had been built in terraced form with stairways providing access to the top. This was the *Castillo* (Spanish for castle or fortress), and though it was grown over with jungle, they could see that it must have been a religious shrine, perhaps a "stairway to the gods."

They couldn't wait to get started! Everywhere about them lay ruins on a grand scale. As quickly as possible they set up quarters at a nearby *hacienda* and started to work.

Not far from their hut, they came upon a long, low building with eighteen thick-walled rooms. In this structure, called by the Indians Akab-Dzib, they discovered an interior doorway that was richly ornamented with hieroglyphs cut carefully in stone.

This seemed odd. These resembled the sculptured writings at Copán and Palenque. Nowhere else in Yucatán had Stephens seen such figures. These designs had been prominent in Guatemala and Honduras; perhaps people from there had emigrated here, founded Chichén Itzá, and had then been conquered by invaders who brought new ideas and designs such as he had noticed at Uxmal. Perhaps it was the invaders who introduced the concepts of war and death's heads and carved reptiles.

Out of the doorway and a few steps through the jungle, they came upon a building of elaborate design and ornamentation. The *Monjas,* they heard it called, and that seemed in keeping, for it was as beautiful as the *Casa de las Monjas* at Uxmal. Stephens was still at a loss to explain the name. The original intent of these buildings, he surmised, had not been housing for nuns.

The building presented a marvelous facade on every side and along the upper story, which was reached by a steep and badly broken stairway. To Catherwood, the end of the building facing the Akab-Dzib was a prize discovery in art as well as architecture, and he drew it in bold designs, as Piranesi had drawn the Roman ruins.

Chichén Itzá: Casa de las Monjas. "It is remarkable for its good state of preservation, and the richness and beauty of its ornaments. . . . It has two cornices of tasteful and elaborate design. Over the doorway are . . . small cartouches of hieroglyphics . . . six bold projecting curved ornaments . . . resembling an elephant's trunk, and . . . an irregular circular niche, in which portions of a seated figure, with a headdress of feathers, still remain . . ." (*Compare with drawing by Catherwood below*)

Chichén Itzá: La Iglesia (the Church). "It is twenty-six feet long, fourteen deep, and thirty-one high, its comparatively great height adding very much to the effect of its appearance. It has three cornices, and the spaces between are richly ornamented. The sculpture is rude but grand. . . . The portion of the facade above the second cornice is merely an ornamental wall."

The wall itself, with but one door, rose twenty-five feet or so above the ground and was, according to Stephens' measurements, thirty-five feet wide. Carved projections extended not only above the doorway but from the corners of the buildings, much as in the *Casa del Gobernador* at Uxmal. Other designs were grotesque and intricate, resembling eerie masks with leering eyes.

Inside they discovered many hidden rooms. In secret passageways, they came upon bats asleep in darkened crevices. Noisy, colorful motmot birds flew chattering in and out of the doorways. In a few places the explorers' torches revealed remains of brightly colored paintings on the walls. Though badly defaced, these paintings still showed portions of human figures whose heads bore plumes of feathers and whose hands held spears and shields.

Almost touching the *Monjas* stood another building called *La Iglesia,* the Church. It, too, had been well ornamented and, while not nearly as large as the *Monjas,* was almost as high. The superstitious Indians told Stephens that every year on Good Friday strange music could be heard in this building. Stephens and Catherwood happened to be in *La Iglesia* on Good Friday, 1842, but heard no music.

Turning to the north and crossing an open field, they came to the oddest ruin of all, a circular building, twenty-two feet in diameter. Only at one other ruin, Mayapán, had they seen a circular building. This one at Chichén Itzá was perched on an elaborate platform to which access was gained by stairways flanked with serpents carved in stone.

What intrigued Stephens most was the spiral staircase inside. In Mexico, such a staircase is called an *escalera de caracol.* This building, therefore, had been named the *Caracol.*

Much of the upper part of the tower was in ruins. Stephens tried to dig his way into passages that were choked with fallen rock, but in the narrow halls could not leap out of the way of stones that he himself dislodged. So he abandoned the enterprise as too dangerous.

If only he had had more time he might have discovered what archeologists later found: evidence that the *Caracol* had been devoted to a study of astronomy.

Stephens did observe that the outer doorways opened exactly to the cardinal points of the compass. Had he been able to climb to the upper portions of the sixty-foot structure, he would have found three openings pointing in very significant directions.

One pointed due south. One marked the place on the

*The Caracol. "Conspicuous among the ruins of Chichén for its pic-
turesque appearance, and unlike any other we had seen . . . it is
circular in form, and is known by the name of the Caracol, or winding staircase, on account of its interior arrangements."*

horizon where the moon set at its farthest south of the year.
The third had a double importance. Viewed from one position, it marked the spot on the horizon where the sun set
at the vernal equinox (March 21), midpoint of its annual
swing between the Equator and the limit of its northern
extension. Viewed from a slightly different angle, this opening fixed for the Maya astronomers a point on the horizon
where the moon set at its farthest north each year.

Unfortunately, Stephens missed all this. The *Caracol* lay
in a state of ruin. Only after archeologists were able to
clean out a good deal of the debris and restore some of the

building did they begin to understand the great achievements of the Mayas.

No matter; Stephens and Catherwood were overwhelmed with what they saw. The giant size and beautiful design of these buildings were marvels enough for them.

Steadily Stephens supervised the Indians in clearing away as many trees and shrubs as possible. Catherwood drew constantly. Yet there were so many temples, so many terraces and fallen buildings, so many mounds and colossal fragments of art. They knew they would never finish.

Beyond the *Caracol* and across the road lay the other half of Chichén Itzá. Here was the *Castillo*, which Stephens called "the grandest and most conspicuous object that towers above the plain."

Grand, indeed! Constructed in the form of a pyramid, it measured approximately 200 feet along each side at the base, and on two sides had stairways leading to the top. No ordinary stairways these, but broad and commanding (forty-four feet wide and containing ninety steps from bottom to top), as if they had been reserved for the most exalted priests to climb.

Great stone serpents, with their tongues protruding, adorned one stairway from top to bottom. How important reptiles must have been in the religion of these ancient people! Stephens remembered the *Casa de Tortugas* at Uxmal, a whole building dedicated to turtles.

Atop the *Castillo* stood the temple they had seen on their approach to Chichén Itzá. Here were doorways with wooden lintels delicately carved—headdresses, plumes, feathers, everything to indicate elaborate ceremonies.

It was an impressive height on which to hold ceremonies of any kind. Inasmuch as Yucatán is mostly flat and forested, this pyramid allowed its builders a view they got in no other way. From the *Castillo* they could see for miles in all directions across the seemingly endless jungle.

*Castillo, Chichén Itzá: (Above) as drawn by Catherwood;
(Below) as it is today*

Temple of the Warriors, Chichén Itzá, showing reclining statue of Chac Mool and, in the distance, the ball court. This temple contains hundreds of columns adorned with a great variety of carvings

"And from this lofty height," Stephens wrote, "we saw for the first time groups of small columns, which, on examination, proved to be among the most remarkable and unintelligible remains we had yet met with. They stood in rows of three, four, and five abreast, many rows continuing in the same direction, when they changed and pursued another. They were very low, many of them only three feet high, while the highest were not more than six feet, and consisted of several separate pieces, like millstones. Many of them had fallen and in some places they lie prostrate in rows, all in the same direction, as if thrown down intentionally.

"I had a large number of Indians at work clearing them, and endeavoring to trace their direction to the end. In some places they extended to the bases of large mounds, on which were ruins of buildings and colossal fragments of sculpture, while in others they branched off and terminated abruptly. I counted 380, and there were many more; but so many were broken and they lay so irregularly that I gave up counting them. They were entirely too low to have supported a roof under which persons could walk. The idea at times suggested itself that they had upheld a raised walk of cement, but there were no remains visible."

This strange compound, with its multitude of square pillars still standing, is now called *Templo de los Guerreros,* or Temple of the Warriors. The colonnades are also referred to as the Court of the Thousand Columns.

You can still see, as Stephens did, the excellent carving on these columns, with their handsome designs of feathered serpents. In front of the main temple rests the stone figure of a man on his back with head and knees upraised. On his

Base of columns at main entrance to the Temple of the Warriors. The heads represent rattlesnakes; the body of each "serpent" forms a column above, and is topped by large carved rattles (not shown)

Gymnasium, or ball court, at Chichén Itzá. In an account of the games played by Mayas here, Stephens wrote: "On the side walls they fixed certain stones, like those of a mill, with a hole quite through the middle, just as big as the ball, and he that could strike it through there won the game."

stomach he holds some sort of bowl. Could this "chac mool," as it is called, have been an altar of sacrifice? At least a dozen such reclining statues have been found at Chichén Itzá. The early Mayas adorned them with pieces of mother-of-pearl or polished bone for eyes, fingernails, and toenails.

As he wandered through these ruins, Stephens had some of his finest hours. He found a ball court, much like one less well preserved at Uxmal. This was larger, with stone rings (we might call them vertical "basketball hoops") in place at the sides. He saw whole walls of stone either painted with reddish pictures and designs, or carved with the finest ceremonial figures.

North of the *Castillo* he found a causeway, really a kind of primitive highway built with stones to provide a reasonably level road through the forest. At the end of this he came upon a large natural well, or *cenote* from the Maya word *dz'onot.*

"The cenote was the largest and wildest we had seen," wrote Stephens. It lay "in the midst of a thick forest, an immense circular hole, with cragged, perpendicular sides, trees growing out of them and overhanging the brink, and still as if the genius of silence reigned within.

"A hawk was sailing around it, looking down into the water, but without flapping its wings. The water was of a greenish hue. A mysterious influence seemed to pervade it, in unison with the historical account that the well of Chichén was a place of pilgrimage and that human victims were thrown into it in sacrifice. In one place, on the very brink, were the remains of a stone structure, probably connected with ancient superstitious rites; perhaps the place from which the victims were thrown into the dark well beneath."

The cenote at Chichén Itzá long remained an intriguing mystery. But eventually a man named Edward Thompson, then United States Consul at Mérida, set to work to solve the mysteries of the sacred well.

Detail of ball court "ring"

"Cenote," or well, at Chichén Itzá. This served not only as a source of water, but as a place where religious ceremonies were held, including the casting of sacrificial victims into the well

Aided by funds from the Peabody Museum of Archeology and Ethnology at Harvard University, Thompson operated a dredge at the *cenote* between 1904 and 1907. During this time he took out a vast quantity of jade objects, pottery, copper and gold pieces, bone and shell carvings, balls of sacred incense, knives, masks, and the skeletal remains of forty-two persons, half of them children. Thompson presented this valuable collection of Maya artifacts to the Peabody Museum.

Several decades later, Mexican scholars began to feel the lack of a study collection from the *cenote* at Chichén Itzá and organized their own expedition. They reasoned that Thompson had found only a fraction of the treasures held by the well. Using modern diving equipment and special lifting devices, the Mexicans, aided by the National Geographic Society, brought up thousands of additional artifacts and more skeletal remains, enough to furnish Mexican archeologists with study material for a long time to come.

Chichén Itzá had overwhelmed Stephens. Here, and in all the other ruins, he tried to search out the hidden meanings of what he saw. "These cities," he wrote, "were not all built at one time, but are the remains of different epochs. Chichén, though in a better state of preservation than most of the others, has a greater appearance of antiquity; some of the buildings are no doubt older than others, and long intervals may have elapsed between the times of their construction."

They certainly had. This great Maya center, archeologists learned later, had been founded in the fifth century, occupied a while, and abandoned in the seventh. In the tenth century it was again occupied, but not for long. It was then reoccupied in the thirteenth century, and has been more or less a place of habitation for the Indians ever since. Stephens had guessed correctly.

Before leaving Yucatán, Stephens, Catherwood, and Cabot rode east to the Atlantic Ocean, and sailed down the coast in a canoe thirty-five feet long and six feet wide. They discovered the ruins of a walled Maya city named Tulum, standing grandly on an eminence overlooking the sea. (See picture on page 49, drawn at Tulum. This is the only

Aerial view of the walled Maya ruin of Tulum, Yucatán, as it is today. "The Castillo rises on the brink of a high, broken, precipitous cliff, commanding a magnificent ocean view, and a picturesque line of coast, being itself visible from a great distance at sea."

San Miguel, Island of Cozumel

known drawing in which Stephens, Catherwood, and Cabot
—at extreme left—appear together.)

They also visited the island of Cozumel, a paradise of
palm trees and shell beaches caressed by gentle tropical
winds.

But at last it was time to go. They returned to Mérida
looking as though they had lived in the wilderness forever
—bearded, dust-covered, disheveled—not a very triumphal
entry, Stephens remarked. In time, they embarked for Cuba
and thence New York.

It was the last time they were to work with Dr. Cabot.
And now that the trip was over, Stephens could see the
wisdom of having selected him as naturalist of the expedition. Cabot had hundreds of bird skins to take back to the
U.S.A., skins that would advance the knowledge of orni-
thology very much indeed.

Dr. Cabot ultimately became one of the finest surgeons
in the United States. He fought doggedly for the abolition
of slavery, married, and became the father of eight chil-

dren, and outlived by far his partners in the Yucatán adventure. He died in 1885.

"In our long, irregular, and devious route," wrote Stephens of his explorations in Yucatán, "we have discovered the crumbling remains of forty-four ancient cities, most of them but a short distance apart. . . . With but few exceptions, all were lost, buried, and unknown, never before visited by a stranger, and some of them, perhaps, never looked upon by the eyes of a white man. . . .

"If I may be permitted to say so, in the whole history of discoveries there is nothing to be compared with those here presented."

SCALE 1: 5,700,000

Statute Miles 25 0 25 50 75

©RAND McNALLY & CO.

To New York

Mérida

YUCATAN

• Mayapan

CHICHÉN ITZÁ RUINS ▲

Kabah

Ticul

Causeway

Cobá ▲

UXMAL RUINS

Sayil

Yaxuná

TULUM RUINS ▲

Isla de Cozumel

1842

1840

GOLFO DE CAMPECHE

CAMPECHE

QUINTANA

ROO

O

C

I

X

C. del Carmen

TABASCO

E

PALENQUE RUINS

Uaxactun •

TIKAL RUINS ▲

BRITISH

CARIBBEAN

M

▲ TONINA RUINS

Río Usumacinta

Laguna de Petén

HONDURAS

SEA

Ococingo

Bonampak

GOLFO DE HONDURAS

Stephens 1840

CHIAPAS

San Andrés

GUATEMALA

Santiago Petatán

Todos Santos

Huehuetenango

Quezaltenango

Chichicastenango

HONDURAS

PACIFIC

L. Atitlán

⊛ Guatemala City

OCEAN

Santiago Atitlán

Antigua

Stephens' route from Guatemala City to the ruins of Palenque, Mexico; from Palenque to the ruins of Uxmal, and home, in 1840; from New York to Uxmal, exploration of Yucatán, and return home, 1841–42

13

THE ANCIENT MAYAS

"SAVAGES never reared these structures," Stephens wrote of the Maya ruins. "Savages never carved these stones."

Since his time a great deal has been learned about the Mayas. Mounds, temples, and cities have revealed secrets, such as those discovered by Alberto Ruz at Palenque, as fabulous as any about which Stephens and Catherwood speculated.

Stephens remained convinced, wherever he went, that this civilization was not a transplanted one—not transplanted from Egypt, or medieval Europe, or China, or from anywhere else. It developed and flourished, he was sure, in the jungles and the highlands of Central America.

Exactly where it started within this region is difficult to say. Archeologists agree that it did not develop as civilizations did in the Old World. There, along the Tigris and Euphrates rivers of Mesopotamia, in what is now Iraq, large populations grew; great cities were built and flourished for centuries. One finds little evidence of that in the Maya region. Many of the temples and "ruined cities" that Stephens explored in Central America were not really cities at all.

As a matter of fact, archeologists find evidence to indicate that many Maya "cities" were more than likely ceremonial centers. The Mayas, then as now, were primarily farmers. Corn was their essence of life, and fields of it were widely spaced in order to make use of the most fertile soil. Hence it is believed that in the lowlands, with some notable exceptions such as Tikal, there were rarely more than thirty

Indian plow

people per square mile—a density of population about the same as today.

But who built the temples and pyramids? Who erected the finely carved monuments, laid out the ball courts, designed the "palaces?"

Among the Mayas, there were probably a few master architects, working out the design of the buildings; a few skillful sculptors chiseling figures in stone; a few teams of laborers hauling in building blocks. Evidence shows that, as at Chichén Itzá, Maya centers were constructed a building at a time, perhaps by several generations of artisans.

What Stephens saw was the accumulation of centuries of work—of design, of carving, of fitting the building blocks in place. To look at all the ruins now, you would think that a large population once spread over this land; but the larger "cities" were probably seldom occupied as homes except by high priests, as we shall see, and were certainly not all built in one generation.

Had Stephens seen Tikal, one of the earliest and largest Maya centers, he might have added another eloquent chapter or two to his books. But Tikal was buried so deeply in the Guatemala jungle that he did not visit it, and perhaps did not even hear of it. Tikal has been dated back as far as A.D. 278 and was a large urban center with a population of at least ten thousand.

Nor did Stephens see Uaxactún, an early Maya center

near Tikal, where an old carved monument, or stela, contains a date equivalent to A.D. 328.

The Maya civilization flourished even before the earliest dates recorded at Tikal. But it is at sites like Tikal and Uaxactún, Copán and Palenque, that we find abundant and spectacular evidence of the early civilization.

Neither Stephens nor Catherwood saw what archeologists later uncovered among the Maya ruins in Guatemala, Honduras, and Mexico. The Mayas carved magnificent objects in jade, a very hard stone. Not having metal tools, they had to resort to such ingenious devices as sawing cord back and forth through grooves, using finely crushed stone as a cutting agent.

Among the Mayas were excellent painters, whose "murals" are outstanding among those of any aboriginal society. Stephens and Catherwood saw a number of painted ceilings, and a few frescoes, but they missed some of the finest wall decorations, such as those at Bonampak, in the forest of Chiapas, Mexico. Virtually every color was used by the

Restored temple at Tikal, largest of Maya cities, in the lowland jungle of Guatemala

Mayas, one so striking that it is known today as Maya blue. The color and design of textiles, if present-day Maya crafts are a basis for judgment, must have been spectacular.

The ancient people made pottery, baskets, mats, and delicate wood carvings. They developed rubber into balls, which the early Spaniards described—thus marking the first European notice of rubber.

The Mayas were not as great road builders as the Incas, but they laid out and constructed excellent highways just the same. Stephens was aware of the causeway between the *Castillo* and the sacred cenote at Chichén Itzá, but not far away lay an even greater highway, the finest Maya road now known. It connects the city of Cobá with a small ruin called Yaxuna. It is sixty-two and one-half miles long, with an average width of thirty-two feet. The early engineers had to lay foundations carefully in swampy land and pack the building materials solidly so that the roadbed would not sag. Today there is no evidence of sagging, after all these centuries.

Added to this is the fact that in going from site to site (or village to village as the case may have been) the road was laid out as straight as an arrow. How the Mayas surveyed it in the depths of the Yucatán jungle, where they could hardly see thirty feet in a straight line, is little short of amazing. The road was built even though the Mayas had no horses or other beasts of burden. They had no wheeled vehicles, either. They never invented or knew about the wheel.

They were good at inventing other things, however, and some of their most enduring inventions are the most striking.

As happens in so many Indian cultures, religion is based upon things important in the growing of crops: earth, sun, rain, and season. If the sun shone too much, drought occurred, crops failed, and famine spread over the land. By elaborate prayers and offerings, many tribes attempted to supplicate the gods of rain and sun. But mortal man had no more ability then than he has now to change the weather or bring on rain.

What he could do, however, indeed *had* to do, was to be sure he got his crops into the ground at the right time. And the only dependable way of telling time from year to year was to observe the revolutions of the sun and moon and other celestial objects. Their motions constituted both clock and calendar.

But the sun did not rise or set in the same place every day. Neither did the moon or the stars. The motions of these heavenly bodies were extremely complicated; whoever mastered them could make predictions about when to plant.

The Mayas mastered them. When it came to astronomy, and to the concept of time, the Mayas made their greatest advances. In several important ways they were ahead of peoples living at about the same time in ancient Greece and Rome.

It wasn't easy. In order to pass on their discoveries to succeeding generations and thus sustain their knowledge, they had first to develop a system of writing, and then a system of mathematics.

This they did, too. Sylvanus Morley, an eminent authority on the Mayas, has said that they were the most civilized people of the New World, in the era before Columbus, because they alone originated a system of writing. Maya writing used hieroglyphic characters to represent ideas. Inscriptions, or "glyphs," that have been translated treat primarily of time, astronomy, and religious matters rather than personal histories. Since Morley's studies, other glyphs have been translated that tell of Maya rulers and when they ruled; still others list the names of cities.

The glyphs the Mayas used for writing were artistic figures or designs that were cut, or carved, or drawn. Some

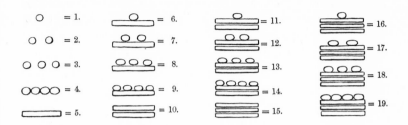

Glyphs of Maya numbers

MONTH SIGNS.

| Pop. | Uo. | Zip. | Tzoz. | Tzec. | Xul. | Yaxkin. | Mol. | Chen. |

| Yax. | Zac. | Ceh. | Mac. | Kankin. | Muan. | Pax. | Kayab. | Cumhu. |

DAY SIGNS.

| Kan. | Chicchan. | Cimi. | Manik. | Lamat. |

| Muluc. | Oc. | Chuen. | Eb. | Ben. |

Glyphs of Maya months and days as published by the British archeologist Alfred Maudslay in 1889 glyphs were simple; some were complex. As far as archeologists can determine, most Maya glyphs represented ideas rather than sounds, although it is possible that many of them are phonetic, or sound, characters (almost two-thirds of these Maya glyphs still remain undecipherable). Among the ideas represented by glyphs were numerous ones that stood for periods of time.

Thanks to the priests and to their study of the motions of heavenly objects, the Mayas developed an uncanny knowledge of the calendar. Twenty days made up their month, and they had eighteen months. One extra month of five days gave them almost a year—365 days in all.

Their days had names (*Imix, Ik, Akbal, Kan,* etc.) and so did the months (*Pop, Uo, Zip, Zotz, Tzec,* etc.). Each day and each month had a written form—a glyph. Their word for day (*kin*), month (*uinal*), and year (*tun*), each had a glyph. And so on for other Maya divisions of time.

The basis for their time calculations was the "movement" of the sun; and yet, the daily apparent movements were not so important. It was the seasons that counted. How long between exact beginnings of spring? How long between the plantings of crops? A few days' error could make a disastrous difference and bring on famine.

Today, with our telescopes and radio clocks, we know that the year is a little longer than 365 days. To be exact, it is 365.2422 days. The Mayas, with no such elaborate equipment, also knew that the year had more than 365 days. Through careful studies (probably by astronomer-priests at Copán) they measured and remeasured the length of the year until they got it down to 365.2420 days!

All this gives but the simplest introduction to the complex subject of Maya astronomy. The ancient astronomers studied and measured with astonishing accuracy the changing positions (we call them revolutions) of the moon. They calculated apparent motions of the planet Venus with such skill that they corrected errors as small as two hours every 584 days. What is more, they developed an intricate system of mathematics to calculate and record these measurements, and invented the concept of the zero before the Greeks and Romans did.

John Lloyd Stephens knew that the Mayas possessed unusual powers of intellect; had he known the things that archeologists later learned, he would have admired them even more.

Where did all this brilliance come from? The first astronomical observatory may have been at Uaxactún, where lines of sight between high temples helped the Mayas fix important calendrical dates such as the vernal equinox and the summer solstice. Although they began to carve their glyphs in stone during the fourth century (our time), they also wrote on wood, or paper, or other perishable materials before that.

Maya books are called *codices,* from the Latin word *codex,* meaning "ancient manuscript," and the "pages" were made from tree bark that was pounded into a pulp and held together with a natural gum. To these long strips of paper was applied, on both sides, a white lime mixture. It was on this surface that the priests inscribed their complex hieroglyphics and painted pictures of their gods and ceremonies, coloring them with vegetable and mineral paints. When finished, the manuscript was folded like a folding screen and placed between wooden or leather covers. Thus was formed a single book, which might unfold to a length of twenty-four feet.

Unfortunately for future scientists, a monk named Diego de Landa arrived in Yucatán in 1549. Landa quickly became convinced that Maya books contained evil and superstitious writings and that the best way to get rid of these ideas was to destroy all the books he could find. So he burned them. This terrible loss has prevented scholars from ever seeing much of the written history of the Mayas, or from deciphering a large part of their hieroglyphic writing.

But Landa didn't get them all. Since his time, three codices, written before the time of Columbus, have been discovered. One, dealing with astronomical calculations, was found in Dresden, Germany. Another book, called the Codex Tro-Cortesianus, found in Spain, concerns the astrology used by Maya priests. Fragments of a third book, found in Paris, France, contain descriptions of some of the Maya deities and religious ceremonies. None of these three books tells anything of Maya history, development, or decline.

What little we do know of the daily life, customs, and history of the Mayas has come down to us from records written by later individuals, who had been taught by the Spanish priests to write the Maya language by using the letters of the Spanish alphabet.

Thus it is evident that the Mayas began early to develop their skills in art, architecture, science, and agriculture, and then passed these skills successfully to each generation for centuries to follow, either by means of written records or by word of mouth.

For this kind of situation to prevail, there must have been very little war. The rulers were probably benevolent, the people contented and free.

Not all their progress was as marked as that in science, but apparently they had enough leisure so that certain groups of men could study the stars and be supported in their work by others. We can only guess. Little record remains of Maya social and political structure.

Despite the hardships of the land in which they lived, the Mayas were able to adapt themselves to jungle life with extraordinary success. Palenque, for example, thrived for some 400 years, which is a remarkably long period when one considers the nature of the jungle, the weather, and the slow progress in other forms of Maya endeavor.

Maya man and boy planting corn

But about A.D. 900 the great religious centers of Copán and Palenque began to decline. It is hard to believe that a civilization so obviously advanced, so apparently peaceful and content, could have collapsed as completely as it did. In a few dozen years, the cities were beginning to crumble into ruin. No more dates were carved, no buildings erected, no sculpture created.

Was this fall of civilization due to earthquakes that sometimes shake the region? Probably not. Was it due to changes in climate that affected the crops? Not very likely. Epidemics of malaria and yellow fever? No; these diseases were brought into the region by Europeans and Africans.

The best answer that archeologists and others can derive from existing knowledge is that the soil "wore out" and

agriculture became difficult, or that the organized priest-
hood fell into disfavor, or that there were Toltec invasions
or threats of invasion from the west. Perhaps the decline
of the Mayas resulted from more than one of these causes.
In the end, the people may have simply grown tired of the
methods used by their masters and either killed the priests
or cast them out. Whatever the cause, the effect was striking. The temples were abandoned and the lands around
them all but deserted.

At this time, however, a new era of Maya culture began
to flourish—in Yucatán. But with a difference.

Stephens recognized the difference between Maya art
at Palenque and at Yucatán. What he didn't know was that
Yucatán had been invaded by members of the Toltec tribe
from farther west in what is now Mexico. Little is known
of these invaders. According to some Maya sources, they
came from the Valley of Mexico (the area around present-
day Mexico City). Within the past fifteen years, excavations
near the Mexican village of Tula, fifty-four miles northwest
of Mexico City, have brought to light a culture so similar
to that preserved at Chichén Itzá that the two cities seem
to have been constructed by the same artists and engineers.
These militaristic invaders were called *Itzás* by the Maya
people.

The Toltecs came equipped with spears to hurl, but no
one is sure that they had to use them. Little is known about
the actual conquest of the original Yucatán Mayas. If it was
not a military conquest, it was almost certainly a religious
one. The Toltecs brought new symbols, new ideas, and new
customs. These were what caught Stephens' eye.

There were great colonnades of carved pillars, like those
at the Temple of the Warriors at Chichén Itzá; round temples like the *Caracol;* designs that included feathered serpents, vultures, jaguars, and row upon row of human skulls;
warrior figures; scenes of human sacrifice in which the heart

*Mural painting of a battle
from the Great Ball Court
Temple at Chichén Itzá*

was cut out and held up to the sun. Copán and Palenque had had some of these things, but not in such prominence.

The Maya founders of Uxmal and Chichén Itzá may not have welcomed all these new designs and ideas, but, as always, they were adaptable. They made the best of the situation.

The invaders from the west moved into Chichén Itzá and Uxmal about the year A.D. 1000. These Yucatán cities flourished with varying degrees of success, as did others, until the middle of the fifteenth century. By that time, the large cities were empty and collapsing into ruin, and the government dissolved. From then on, the people were more or less under regional chieftains, and it was these groups that the Spaniards first met as they sailed along the coast of Yucatán.

Perhaps it was just as well. The change of empires was inevitable, for the Mayas had no weapons to match those of the Spaniards.

But the Mayas still live in Yucatán and in Guatemala and, in fact, over much of the land they have occupied since time immemorial. In many respects, they have changed from the kind of people their ancestors were. Today they can obtain what the ancient Mayas never had: such things as transportation by bus, a great variety of ready-made threads and woven fabrics, tin cups, radios, sewing machines, and assorted objects that can be purchased in stores or at village squares on market day.

Modern Mayas are a short, coppery-brown people, whose features resemble those carved in many a ruin. They are of commendable honesty and rare good humor. They do not eat much, but they are hard workers. In the hill country of Guatemala they may be seen transporting on their backs such large loads of firewood or pottery as would stagger a less sturdy people. In their small towns and villages of

Maya boys at Lake Atitlán, Guatemala

thatch-roofed huts, they still speak the Maya language, and still carry on some of the religious practices of old. They are superstitious, but intelligent, skillful in arts and crafts, and generally inclined to follow the habits and customs of their ancestors.

Yet if there is one thing that dominates their life—as it dominated the lives of their forebears for the past three thousand years or more—it is corn. Maya men burn and clear the jungle in order to establish cornfields. This is no small task when you consider that the ancient Mayas had no metal at all with which to manufacture axes and saws. They did very well, however, in clearing, fencing, weeding, and harvesting with stone axes and other tools.

Corn today provides nearly eighty-five per cent of the Mayas' food, and this was probably also true of the prehistoric Mayas. Many is the time that Stephens and Catherwood had to subsist on corn in its various forms. In those days you had to eat tortillas—the flat baked cakes of ground cornmeal—or you got very hungry indeed.

The Mayas had other foods, including beans, squash, breadnut, honey, mamey, cacao, papaya, guava, avocado, and even chewing gum. Still, as Sylvanus Morley says, "With all this abundance, nature's richest gift was maize, without which the Maya could not have developed their distinctive culture, the most brilliant aboriginal civilization of the New World."

Making tortillas

14

PANAMA

EARLY in 1843, Stephens' new book, *Incidents of Travel in Yucatán*, was published. It was evidently what the public was waiting for, because it was an immediate success.

It required a good deal of hard work, because Stephens was scrupulously careful. He looked up and entered page after page of facts and background to make the story of his travels more understandable and complete. Like his earlier book, *Incidents of Travel in Central America, Chiapas & Yucatán*, this new one was big enough to make two volumes.

William H. Prescott, whose own monumental work, *The Conquest of Mexico*, was published during the fall of the same year, wrote to Stephens that this new book was even better than the last. The public scooped up copies as fast as they could be printed, which was again and again as new editions rolled off the press. The work was subsequently issued in England and then translated and published in Mexico, France, Germany, and Sweden.

Bathed with success after this enormous task, Stephens took time out for what was almost surely his second favorite occupation—politics. Using his fame, his ability to speak and write, and his smooth demeanor, he joined the campaign to get James Polk elected President. To his great delight, Polk succeeded. And just as the Guatemaltecos feared, Texas was annexed by the United States of America. Not long after came war with Mexico.

Catherwood was busy, too. After publishing a collection of drawings, he went to British Guiana to help build a railroad. He had long been interested in civil engineering, and had studied it on his own. Now he had a chance to put his knowledge to work.

Stephens, still restless, turned from archeology and politics to commercial ventures. He helped to pioneer steamship navigation across the Atlantic at a time when steam was beginning to replace wind and sail as a means of propulsion. A milestone of his career occurred in Germany, where he succeeded in meeting one of his heroes, Alexander von Humboldt, the famous naturalist, diplomat, geographer, and archeologist.

If there is one thing that stands out about John Lloyd Stephens, it is his astuteness in selecting projects on which to devote his time and earnings. He had an uncanny way of determining the future importance of things, and almost never allied himself with lost causes. His books, for example, were so adroitly written that they are as exciting and readable today as they were more than a century ago.

His final venture took him south at a time when the United States was gripped with gold rush fever. The discovery of gold in the soon-to-be-annexed state of California confirmed in Stephens' mind what he had known for a long time: the U.S.A. must find a quick and easy route for the transport of goods and passengers from the eastern states to the western. As yet there were no transcontinental railroads, or even surveys for them. A vast mid-continent barrier of mountain, plain, and desert lay between New York and California, a land inhabited by Indians, traders, trappers, and wild animals.

To Stephens the answer was simple: go by ship!

Why not cross the continent at its narrowest place, the Isthmus of Panama? It was the old question of a canal again.

Ship captains had to guide their vessels down to the

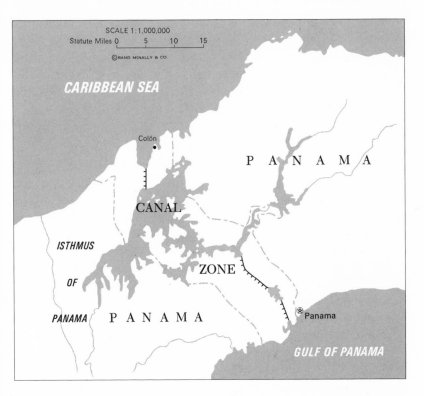

southern tip of South America, there to battle storms and
mountainous waves and fierce winds through the Straits of
Magellan, risking their lives and cargoes in the process, and
then sail thousands of miles to the north along the Pacific
Coast. What a waste of time and money!

A canal where the continents met would save not only
days of time but millions of dollars. The distance from New
York to San Francisco around Cape Horn was 13,000 miles.
Via the Isthmus of Panama it was 5,600. Obviously, cutting
a channel through would be worth almost any price. If
such a task had seemed to Stephens too formidable in Nicaragua earlier, perhaps it was possible in Panama now.

After all, the Isthmus was only fifty miles across at its narrowest. Certainly a canal that long could be built.

The land belonged to Colombia, then known as the Republic of New Granada, and that country knew very well what an asset a canal would be. Colombian officials had begun as early as the 1830's to negotiate with world powers for the building of a canal. The French tried more than once, but had to give up, and the whole idea was abandoned. Fifty miles of jungle and mountain were too much for the times.

Yet there was a way. Railroads had lately been successful in the United States. Why not a railroad across the Isthmus? Vessels from New York could be unloaded on the Atlantic side, their cargo shipped by rail to Pacific ports, loaded into other vessels, and shipped to the final destination.

To Stephens this seemed to be a splendid idea. Practical as he was, he saw that where a canal had failed, a railroad might be built. And the United States, with all its knowledge of railway engineering, ought to be able to do it.

Although France had secured an option to build and operate a railroad, another internal revolution broke out and France's hopes collapsed. Then, in 1848, with the discovery of gold in California, the rush was on, and the following year would see the annexation of California as a state. Being a two-ocean nation, the United States now needed a maritime link between east and west. The answer was Panama, even if the Isthmus had to be crossed by rail. Later, perhaps, there could be a canal.

Humboldt had seen the wisdom of an Isthmus crossing. And many years before, the famous German poet, Goethe, had written, "It is absolutely indispensable for the United States to effect a passage from the Mexican Gulf to the Pacific Ocean; and I am certain that they will do it. Would that I might live to see it!"

Getting to work, Stephens stimulated the organization

of a Panama Railroad Company, and went to Panama to survey the route. On his return, he petitioned Congress for financial help in the enterprise but was rebuffed by President Polk himself. Polk thought of the Panama railroad as a scheme to plunder the Treasury.

Undaunted, Stephens continued surveying, and found a much lower mountain pass than any previously explored—making the railroad even more possible. Working with private resources, he started gathering men and equipment.

The first transcontinental railroad was under way!

At this point, Stephens called for advice from a man who by now knew more about railroad building in the tropics than anyone else—Frederick Catherwood.

In British Guiana, Catherwood's railway project had not succeeded very well (only eight miles of railway were completed), but it was the first railway in South America, and Catherwood had accumulated a wealth of experience in all the trials and tribulations of working in the tropics.

So the red-haired New Yorker and the British architect

"Running the lines." Surveying for the Panama Railway often had to be done through swampy lands

John Lloyd Stephens, at age 40, about the time
he was appointed president of the Panama Railway

joined forces once again. But this time it was on the Río
Chagres, and this time there was no Mico Mountain to
cross on muleback.

Stephens persuaded Catherwood to take over the ad-
ministration of the railway project temporarily, and shortly
afterwards left for Bogotá, capital of the Republic, to ar-
range for a railroad contract.

It was on this trip, after all his thousands of miles of

travel in Central America, that he was finally injured in an accident. High on a trail in the Andes, near Bogotá, his mule became frightened and pitched him off. He fell with great violence against a rock and struck his back so hard that a piece of vertebra was chipped, paralyzing his legs.

It was an extremely painful experience, but it didn't stop the seemingly unstoppable Stephens.

He had to be carried on a palanquin, but he went on to Bogotá and completed the negotiations. At that time, Colombian officials were only too happy to have a United States company involved. They feared that the British might seize a part of the province of Panama and use it themselves as a site for building a canal.

Having completed his negotiations, Stephens returned to New York, and soon had improved enough to walk. He was elected president of the Panama Railway Company and, when he returned to Panama in August, 1850, work was moving along. Slowly, through steaming, insect-infested jungles, the rails were being laid, from the island of Manzanillo up the Chagres River. At the same time, another crew was starting inland from the Pacific Ocean side of the Isthmus.

And yet, alas, it seemed as if the railroad would meet the fate of all other schemes for conquest of this narrow neck of land. The whole project had turned out to be extremely expensive the farther they went, and the company's funds began to run low. Diseases had taken toll of the workmen. And disease was stalking Stephens as well. His old familiar enemy, malaria, racked him more and more often and laid him low in his little cottage on the banks of the Chagres.

Luckily for the sagging fortunes of the company, however, large numbers of people had begun to arrive on their way to the gold fields of California. They were in a hurry to get to the gold and they demanded passage on the short length of the railway that had been completed. For a price they got it.

Thanks to this profit-making venture, the company was beginning to pull out of its slump. Once again the rails went forward as steadily as it was possible to lay them.

Then Catherwood began to succumb to the ills of the tropics and finally became too ill to continue his work. In November, 1850, Stephens accompanied him to Panama City, where he embarked upon a vessel to California. They said good-by, and one may imagine that it was the kind of sad and brave farewell between men whose friendship had been deep and abiding for many years and through many adventures, and who suspected that they were never to see each other again.

Stephens' cottage on the Río Chagres, Panama

The farther the railroad went, the worse Stephens' health became. He shivered miserably as chills possessed and shook him. High fever racked his body as it had so often before. The malaria attacks were increasing in frequency.

Now, however, there was a difference. The strain was beginning to tell. Forty-six eventful years had left their mark. He had done so much, lived so fully, walked so much, ridden so far, dug into ruins, studied, written, suffered diseases. No man is an engine. He was simply worn out, battered by malaria and internal ailments, aggravated from years in the tropics. He had not cared for himself as a wife might have cared for him. He never married. He was too busy and too curious. Now, the state of medicine being what it was, little could be done to repair or revitalize his tortured body. Quinine had been discovered to lessen malarial fevers, and although he consumed large doses of the bitter drug, it was too late to have any effect.

Eventually, on the verge of death, he was taken from Panama to New York City.

There, on September 22, 1852, the very day that a ship bearing his name—the S.S. *John L. Stephens*—was launched, he fell into a coma.

It was his last fight. He lay unconscious for more than three weeks, and finally died on October 13.

"I take my leave of the reader," he had said in one of his books. "I have carried him over seas and rivers, mountains and plains, through royal palaces and peasants' huts, and in return for his kindness in accompanying me to the end, I promise that I will not again burden him with my *Incidents of Travel*."

No burden at all. His four separate works titled *Incidents of Travel* endured for many years, and delighted hundreds of thousands of readers. Two of them—the volumes on Central America and Yucatán—are still in print and still in

"Stephens was found unconscious under a huge liana-draped ceiba tree near Lion Hill beyond Gatun Station. The natives who found him at first thought him dead. . . . As they bore him away limp and unconscious to a vessel leaving for New York, rumor had it that he was dead. For fifty years this tree was called 'Stephens' Tree', for legend, more persistent than truth, had it that John Lloyd Stephens . . . died under the ceiba tree," said Stephens' biographer. The original layout of the road involved destruction of the tree, but so greatly was Stephens admired that a diversion of the line was ordered to save the tree

demand for their rousing adventure, their wit and good humor, and their array of historic information.

Largely owing to Stephens' pioneering efforts, work on the Panama railroad continued and, in 1855, just three years after his death, it was completed. The village where it began grew rapidly into a city that was named Colón, the Spanish way of saying Columbus. The town on the Pacific side was called simply Panama.

The railroad was so successful that, ten years after its completion, it had earned more than it originally cost to build, which was $8,000,000. It was, at the time, considered the most successful endeavor ever undertaken outside the United States. In 1877 it was sold to the French Panama Canal Company for $25,000,000. Stephens had indeed known what he was doing!

After this, the French did the best they could to build a canal across the Isthmus. But there was corruption in the company, and the old specter of tropical disease still lingered. Besides, the job was so enormous that it presented an insurmountable challenge to the men and equipment of the times.

The French dug out seventy-six million cubic yards of earth, but by 1889 they were bankrupt, and the canal project was abandoned once again.

The United States had not lost interest, and Congress soon authorized a new survey of possible routes for a canal. Nicaragua was recommended as a site, because a canal there, though longer, would require less digging. However, the French had already made a start in Panama. A great deal of earth had already been removed. Furthermore, the French were willing to sell their interest in the scheme.

During subsequent negotiations, the province of Panama revolted from Colombia and declared its independence. In 1903 the United States concluded a treaty with the new

Terminus of the Panama Railway, below Panama City

nation for the construction and operation of a canal.

The work now moved ahead in earnest, and, as the years passed, the threat of dread diseases, such as yellow fever, bubonic plague, and malaria, diminished.

This time, as John Lloyd Stephens had predicted so long ago, the job was done.

A canal at last! In 1914, the first ship went through and, in 1920, the canal was proclaimed officially open.

How pleased Stephens would have been to see the finished canal. His dream had become a reality. It had been eighty years since he published Baily's measurements of a proposed Nicaraguan canal.

"As yet," he wrote in his *Incidents of Travel in Central America, Chiapas, & Yucatán*, "the subject . . . has not taken any strong hold upon the public mind. It will be discussed, frowned upon, sneered at, and condemned as visionary and impracticable. Many in established business will oppose it as deranging the course of their trade. Capitalists will not risk their money in an unsettled and revolutionary country. The pioneers will be denounced and ridiculed, as Clinton was when he staked his political fortunes upon the 'big ditch' that was to connect the Hudson with Lake Erie.

"But if the peace of Europe be not disturbed, I am persuaded that the time is not far distant when the attention of the whole civilized and mercantile world will be directed toward it, and steamboats will give the first impulse. In less than a year, English mailboats will be steaming to Cuba, Jamaica, and the principal ports of Spanish America, touching once a month at San Juan and Panama.

"To men of leisure and fortune, jaded with rambling over the ruins of the Old World, a new country will be opened. After a journey on the Nile, a day in Petra, and a bath in the Euphrates, English and American travelers will be bitten by mosquitoes on the Lake of Nicaragua, and will drink champagne and Burton ale on the desolate shores of San Juan on the Pacific. The random remarks of the traveler for amusement, and the observations of careful and scientific men, will be brought together, a mass of knowledge will be accumulated and made public, and in my opinion the two oceans will be united."

And so they were. But it was something Stephens did not live to see.

Frederick Catherwood did not see it either. After leaving Stephens in Panama in 1850, Catherwood spent several years in California and then went back to England. In 1854, he set out on the first leg of his return to California aboard the S.S. *Arctic,* bound for New York with 385 passengers aboard. The initial landfall was to have been Newfoundland, but on the day they were scheduled to dock there, the ship drifted into fog.

Suddenly, out of the mists, bearing directly upon the *Arctic,* came a French vessel by the name of *Vesta.* There was no avoiding it: the two ships collided head-on with a terrific crash. The *Arctic* went to the bottom, along with nearly every one of its passengers, including Frederick Catherwood.

15

THE RUINS TODAY

THE appearance of many of the ruins has vastly changed since Catherwood drew them and Stephens wrote about them in the 1840's. Where the two explorers saw trees growing from sprawling mounds, now archeologists have excavated and stabilized a few of the shattered buildings. Some ruins have been partially restored.

To the countries concerned, these prehistoric sites are an immensely important part of the national heritage and a source of pride and profit. An arm of the military forces of the Republic of Honduras (*Cuerpo Militar*) exercises strict control over the use of the ruins of Copán. An archeological museum has been established in the village of Copán and visitors may see some of the finest and most significant objects unearthed from the ruins.

Nowadays, you may reach the ruins of Copán over a difficult mountain road, hazardous of passage in the rainy season. Or you may get there by chartering a light aircraft, which will land you on a simple field within a hundred yards of the ruins.

Entering the forest that still grows over the outlying mounds, you sense some of the thrill of expectation that Stephens and Catherwood must have felt on their first trip across the Copán River to the ruins. The central part of the great site stands in contrast to the gloom of the woods. In the open sunlit plazas, the ruins now are cleared, and some of them have been partially excavated and restored. Silent white walls and intricately carved stelae shine brilliantly in the tropical sunlight.

Copán ruins in Honduras. At center, the ball court; in the distance, the plaza of the stone monuments; lower right, part of hieroglyphic stairway

As you walk among the temples of a bygone age, few creatures—mostly iguanas—move in the shadows. The human ghosts of the Mayas are silent and invisible, but the works of these early Indians endure, and the spirit of their genius is all about you. The Hieroglyphic Stairway is there, but no one now is permitted to climb it, lest the delicate carvings made so long ago by ancient man be damaged or destroyed by modern man.

The plazas, courtyards, grand staircases, sculptured heads, and ornate altars have been rescued from the earth or from the ravages of time. They, more than anything else, testify to the artistry and perseverance of the builders of this ancient civilization.

Far across the rugged mountains, sparkling streams still pour into the silt-laden Motagua River, which winds through the desert country of Guatemala as peacefully as during

Aerial view of Guatemala City

Stephens' visit. The pitching hillsides, down which water-falls cascade through forests of pine, or palm, or thick jungle, rise up in peaks that frequently are lost in the clouds.

Guatemala City is a thriving metropolis of more than half a million people, with plazas, markets, and gardens much like those that Stephens thought so interesting.

The troubled days of Morazán and Carrera are but spirited adventures on the pages of Central American history. Morazán returned from exile in 1842 in a last-ditch attempt to save the *Provincias Unidas del Centro de América* (United States of Central America) but did not succeed and died before a firing squad in September of that year.

Carrera ruled Guatemala, and dominated neighboring countries, until his death in 1865. But history grants to Morazán the honors of greatness, and Central Americans—especially in his homeland of Honduras—have erected numerous monuments to him. He is deemed to have been a freedom fighter in the best tradition, and historians now regard as a catastrophe Carrera's revolt against Morazán and the destruction of the fledgling United States of Central America.

The road Stephens followed from Guatemala City to Lake Atitlán is paralleled by the modern Pan American Highway. The extraordinary scenic grandeur is still there, and the land retains the charm and warmth and interest that Stephens described.

The volcanoes still rise gently from the shore of Lake Atitlán to reach majestic heights. The water remains a deep rich blue and green. Red-roofed huts are gathered in villages around the edges of the lake or perched on slopes of the crater walls. It is easy to understand what Stephens meant when he said, "From the moment this lake first opened upon us until we left it, our ride along it presented a greater combination of beauties than any locality I ever saw."

Palenque, which Stephens and Catherwood had such trouble getting to, can now be reached by train. The Palace Group remains one of the most outstanding collections of buildings in the land of the Mayas, giving this site the air of a monument to the architecture of the ancients. Wandering through the ruins today, one can almost see, as Stephens did, the great temples occupied as they once were.

Native canoes at Lake Atitlán, showing village of Santiago Atitlán and volcano

What heights our imagination lifts us to! "We lived in the ruined palace of their kings," Stephens had written. "We called back into life the strange people who gazed at us in sadness from the walls; pictured them, in fanciful costumes and adorned with plumes of feathers, ascending the terraces of the palace and the steps leading to the temples. . . . In the romance of the world's history nothing ever impressed me more forcibly than the spectacle of this once great and lovely city, overturned, desolate, and lost. . . ."

Palenque is no longer lost. Nor are Uxmal and Chichén Itzá. In this modern world these wonderful ruins lie mere hours away by jet. Yet they are in the midst of jungles that the ancient Maya Indians occupied for centuries. The ruins, the jungle, perhaps even the people themselves, are little changed from that other distant world of long ago.

Today we can discover for ourselves the unfading fascination of the Maya ruins. It was that fascination that drew John Lloyd Stephens and Frederick Catherwood on, searching for the wonders of Central America.

Perhaps the trail over Mico Mountain is still there, though the monkeys are doubtless rarer now and less often heard in howling choruses in the trees.

The shouts of the old muleteers, *"Ho, mula! Ándale!"* are gone forever. And only in our imagination can we see the red-haired New Yorker, mud-splashed and bedraggled, smiling dryly as he listened to his companion say: "If I had known of this mountain, you might have come to Central America alone!"

FOR FURTHER READING

Catherwood, Frederick, *Views of Ancient Monuments in Central America, Chiapas, & Yucatán*, 1844, Bartlett and Welford Co., New York; republished in 1965 by Barre Publishers, Barre, Massachusetts.

Gallenkamp, Charles, *Maya: The Riddle and Rediscovery of a Lost Civilization*, 1959, David McKay & Co., New York; republished in paperback in 1962 by Pyramid Publications, Inc., New York.

Lavine, Harold, *Central America*, 1964, Time, Inc., New York.

Morley, Sylvanus G., *The Ancient Maya*, 1946, Stanford University Press, Stanford, California.

Stephens, John L., *Incidents of Travel in Arabia Petraea*, 1837, Harper Bros., New York.

Incidents of Travel in Greece, Turkey, Russia, & Poland, 1838, Harper Bros., New York.

Incidents of Travels in Central America, Chiapas, & Yucatán, 1841, Harper Bros., New York; republished in 1949 by Rutgers University Press, New Brunswick, N.J.

Incidents of Travel in Yucatán, 1843, Harper Bros., New York; republished in 1962 by the University of Oklahoma Press, Norman, Oklahoma; and, in a paperback edition, in 1963 by Dover Books, New York.

Thompson, J. Eric S., *The Rise and Fall of Maya Civilization,* 1954, University of Oklahoma Press, Norman, Oklahoma.

Von Hagen, Victor, *Frederick Catherwood, Archt.,* 1950, Oxford University Press, New York.

Maya Explorer: John Lloyd Stephens and the Lost Cities of Central America and Yucatán, 1947, University of Oklahoma Press, Norman, Oklahoma.

The Ancient Sun Kingdoms of the Americas, 1957, World Publishing Company, Cleveland.

PICTURE CREDITS

Pages 14 and 108, Courtesy of the American Museum of Natural History; pages 19, 23, 57, 63, 66, 97, 169, 173, 179, 182, and 187 are reproduced from the collections of the Library of Congress; pages 31, 32, 36, 39, 41, 42, 44, 49, 84, 113, 115, 135 (top), 148, 153 (bottom), 158 (top), 161, 162, and 165 are from Catherwood drawings or lithographs, reproduced from the collections of the Library of Congress; pages 33 and 120 (photos by Carnegie Institute), 47 (photo by United Fruit Co.), 74 (photo by Pan American Airways), 112 (photo by Mexican Tourist Dep't), and pages 78, 87, 163, and 197 courtesy of Pan American Union; pages 53, 54, 60, and 198 courtesy of Guatemala Tourist Bureau (photos by Rodolfo Reyes Juarez); pages 68, 69, 102, and 200 courtesy of Pan American Airways; page 93 is from The Bettmann Archive; pages 118, 156, 164, and 177 are photographs by Matilda Metcalf; page 121, courtesy of National Museum of Anthropology, Mexico City; page 170 is a photograph by Jorge Ibarra; pages 188, 190, 192, and 194 are from engravings in *Harper's Monthly Magazine,* January, 1859, reproduced from the collections of the Library of Congress. All pictures not mentioned above are photographs by Ann and Myron Sutton.

Maps were prepared especially for this book by Rand McNally & Co.

INDEX, PRONUNCIATIONS, and DEFINITIONS

(Figures in **bold face** indicate pictures)

Printed in U.S.A.